Praise for *The Divorce Hacker's Guide*

"Ann Grant's legal, financial, and psychological expertise helps the reader skillfully prepare and protect herself as she navigates the messy minefield of a modern divorce — proactively, efficiently, resiliently. Grant's detailed tips guide the reader step-by-step through the practical nuts and bolts of recruiting resources and developing parenting and employment/business plans, all the while healing the grief and sustaining genuine well-being. *The Divorce Hacker's Guide to Untying the Knot* is terrific; it's the quintessential road map for meeting change with courage and developing the skills to create a new life."

— **Linda Graham, MFT,** author of *The Resilience Toolkit: Powerful Practices for Bouncing Back from Disappointment, Difficulty, and Even Disaster*

"In *The Divorce Hacker's Guide to Untying the Knot*, Ann Grant encourages divorcing women to 'be *better*, not bitter.' With her compassionate and levelheaded advice, she shows you how to reclaim your power, cultivate well-being, and forge a path to a better life."

— **Christine Hassler,** author of *Expectation Hangover*

"Wow! This is *the* comprehensive guide to everything you need to know about surviving a divorce with your sanity in check and your checkbook intact. Ann Grant's help starts from the time you suspect there *may* be a problem in your relationship and carries right through to settling into your next chapter. Her advice is wise, her examples are relatable, and her book is a must-read before, during, and after the uncoupling process."

— **Lois P. Frankel, PhD,** author of *Nice Girls Don't Get Rich* and *Nice Girls Don't Get the Corner Office*

the DIVORCE HACKER'S guide to UNTYING the KNOT

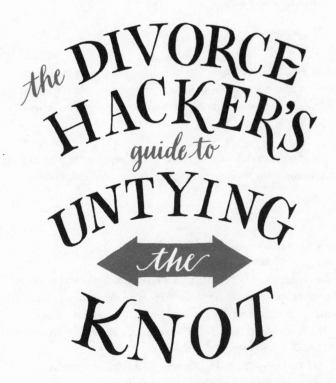

the DIVORCE HACKER'S guide to UNTYING the KNOT

What Every Woman Needs to Know
about Finances, Child Custody,
Lawyers, and Planning Ahead

ANN E. GRANT, JD

New World Library
Novato, California

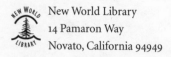

New World Library
14 Pamaron Way
Novato, California 94949

Text design by Tona Pearce Myers

Library of Congress Cataloging-in-Publication Data
Names: Grant, Ann E., author.
Title: The divorce hacker's guide to untying the knot : what every woman needs to know
    about finances, child custody, lawyers, and planning ahead / Ann E. Grant, JD.
Description: Novato, California : New World Library, 2018. | Includes index.
Identifiers: LCCN 2018020151 (print) | LCCN 2018020892 (ebook) | ISBN 9781608685615
    (ebook) | ISBN 9781608685608 (alk. paper)
Subjects: LCSH: Divorce—Law and legislation—United States—Popular works. |
    Divorce—Law and legislation—California—Popular works. | Divorced women—
    United States—Handbooks, manuals, etc.
Classification: LCC KF535.Z9 (ebook) | LCC KF535.Z9 G733 2018 (print) |
    DDC 346.7301/66—dc23
LC record available at https://lccn.loc.gov/2018020151

First printing, September 2018
ISBN 978-1-60868-560-8
Ebook ISBN 978-1-60868-561-5

Printed in Canada on 100% postconsumer-waste recycled paper

New World Library is proud to be a Gold Certified Environmentally Responsible Publisher. Publisher certification awarded by Green Press Initiative.
www.greenpressinitiative.org

10   9   8   7   6   5   4   3   2   1

This book is dedicated to every woman who is struggling in an unfulfilling marriage and doesn't know what to do. I hope that in these pages you find the courage and wisdom to take whatever action is required to lead a satisfying life — and to take back your power.

Contents

Introduction

*N*ot long ago, I was in your shoes. I experienced the demise of my marriage, and it felt as though my life was over. Everything that I had dreamed of came to an abrupt end, and on the worst days, I literally didn't know how I was going to make it through. I was sick, scared, and felt constantly under attack from my soon-to-be ex-husband and overwhelmed by the divorce proceedings as our marriage unraveled. I didn't know where to turn.

In time, I learned that life could be better — much, much better. By combining my practical skills as a lawyer and an empowering healing practice, I found a way out of the chaos to take back my power and create a new and better life. In this book, I share what I learned with you, so that you, too, can create the life of your dreams. Divorce does not have to be the end of your life, and it does not have to be an endless, complicated undertaking. It is an opportunity for a new and better life, and I am here to show you how to make that a reality.

The First Essential Truth

Let's start first with an essential truth: You cannot depend on your husband anymore to look out for your best interests. It is astounding how many women walk through the doors of my legal practice believing that, even as they are going through divorce, their husband can be trusted to "do the right thing" for them. These women assume that, since they are trying to "do the right thing," their husband will do so as well. Every woman I have represented has experienced that "aha" moment of awareness — that he's no longer looking out for you. This isn't "man-bashing." There are plenty of good and honest fellows out there. But it is a fact that, during a divorce, the man who once promised to put you first is no longer doing that. The sooner you accept this inconvenient truth, the sooner you will be on your way to regaining your power and building a better life.

Like so many women, I gave up a lot of power to my husband during our marriage. I let him handle the finances and trusted him to look out for the family's best interest, including mine and that of our three children. In my twenties and thirties, I worked as a litigator at a big corporate law firm, but I gave up my career to raise the kids. My husband — also a lawyer — did very well, and we had a good life. We lived in a beautiful beachside town, belonged to a private country club, and took vacations to Hawaii and ski trips with our friends. After sixteen years of marriage, however, things began to change — and I chose to ignore the signs because I wanted everything to continue just as it was. As things worsened, I did what most women do: took my husband to a marriage counselor, hoped for the best, and let him continue to handle our finances the way he always had.

I want you to know that virtually every woman who has walked through the doors of my office has had some version of this same story: "We just didn't want to see the truth about what was happening, and then one day it was too late." In the legal world this is called "willful blindness."

In my case, my willful blindness ended late one Tuesday night in April, a few weeks after our son's baseball team, coached by my husband, won the Little League championship, and we hosted a wonderful party for all the kids and team parents. Late that Tuesday night, I learned that my marriage was broken beyond repair. After two years in marriage counseling, I finally came to the realization that we could no longer remain married, although I loved him deeply and wanted nothing more than to save our marriage.

I tell this story to let you know that if you are in the same place — going to weekly meetings with a therapist, holding on to the hope of saving your marriage, carrying on life as usual but knowing in your heart that your husband is not fully committed — you are putting yourself and your family at risk. It's time to pull off the Band-Aid, face the truth, and take proactive steps to protect yourself and move forward. There is a way out, and I will show you how in this book.

The Second Essential Truth

The second essential truth is that you cannot blindly depend on divorce "professionals" to look out for your best interest. Many lawyers, accountants, and even some therapists make the divorce process a lot more complicated and drawn out than it needs to be. This is no accident, because they get paid by the hour. These people have zero incentive for you to quickly wrap things up and move on with your life. The longer you are tied up with your divorce and the more you fight, the longer and more you will be paying them. A divorce can drag on for years and cost thousands of dollars more than it should while the "professionals" line their pockets.

Of course, there are divorce professionals with high standards and integrity, and I will show you how to find them. Armed with the knowledge of how the system *really* works, you will be positioned to know who has your best interests in mind and who doesn't. The fact is that most divorces are not that complex. If you can make a human in nine months, you can untie the knot in less time.

The Third Essential Truth

The third essential truth is that you cannot rely for advice on Aunt Martha from Chicago who got divorced back in 1983 or on your friend from college whose husband is a patent attorney. Although well intentioned, friends and family members can steer you in the wrong direction, and the unintended consequences can be emotionally and financially devastating.

Who can you trust? Where can you turn? *The Divorce Hacker's Guide to Untying the Knot*. In these pages, I show you how to take action so that you can create a new and better life with your sanity intact and your money in the bank. I've created a program that *works*. I offer up the same insider information I deliver to my clients every day: truthful advice about legal, financial, custody, real estate, and career issues, plus compassionate guidance for caring for children, healing emotional wounds, and regaining your power.

Wellness is an essential part of my program for getting through your divorce with your sanity intact, and it is absolutely indispensable to creating a new and better future. My divorce was nastier and messier than *Kramer vs. Kramer*. In spite of that, I learned how to access the power within in order to move forward and eventually coparent with my ex. If I could do it, I assure you that you can, too. In this book, as I walk through each step in the legal process, I also walk you through some simple yet powerful strategies for healing your emotional wounds, so that when the divorce decree is entered, you are ready to start your new life from a place of strength and self-worth.

Using a checklist approach to simplify what you need to do and when to do it, *The Divorce Hacker's Guide* outlines each step in the legal process from the decision to file through the final judgment. It addresses all the things you must consider in six key areas — legal, financial, career, children, home, and well-being — and breaks them down into manageable tasks so that nothing falls through the cracks and you aren't overwhelmed. Look for these icons throughout the book:

Legal   Financial   Career   Children   Home   Well-Being

Certain steps in the legal process are common to every divorce: filing and responding to the petition, preparing financial disclosures, engaging in settlement negotiations, and preparing the final judgment of dissolution. The book takes a chronological approach to working through these common legal tasks, but don't hesitate to jump in wherever you are in the process. My goal, by dividing the book into clearly defined topics, is to help you easily customize the advice to serve your unique situation, so you find the information you need. For example, if you have kids, look for the children icon; if you don't, skip those sections. Need to know what to do right now about your house? Look for the home icon in each chapter to answer your questions.

Successfully re-creating yourself through divorce requires more than just navigating the legal process. *The Divorce Hacker's Guide* takes the guesswork out of such difficult questions as "Should I, or can I, keep my house?" "When do I tell the kids about the divorce, and what do I tell them?" and "When should I get back to work, and how can I use my divorce to start a new career or launch a business?"

Throughout, "Insider Tips" take the mystery out of divorce — for example, revealing the real reason your husband wants you to mediate and why he is suddenly insisting on spending more time with the kids. *The Divorce Hacker's Guide* reveals the secrets some divorce professionals don't want you to know — and how to avoid the traps that can cause your case to drag on so that they can keep billing you.

In conjunction with this book, check out the DivorceHacker app (available on my website, www.thedivorcehacker.com, and through Apple's App Store), which is a handy tool that can guide you through the same steps as the book and that provides easy-to-use checklists when you're on the go. In the app, select the icons that apply to your situation, and as you work through them, the app will show you where you are on track and where you need to focus more time and energy to reach your goals.

You can create the life you choose if you implement this program and follow these steps.

CHAPTER I

Preparing to Get What You Need

"A crisis is a gift, an opportunity, and perhaps a manifestation that life loves us, by beckoning us to go beyond the dance we presently perform."

— Leslie Lebeau

*A*s soon as you learn that your marriage is in trouble, take some key steps to protect yourself. While you may be hoping that things will work out, there is simply no substitute for being prepared in the event that they don't. Do not be lulled into complacency if you are working with a marriage counselor or clergy in an effort to save your marriage; don't expect that things will somehow magically get better if you wait long enough for your husband to "come around." While it's fine to hope for the best, you need to *prepare for the worst*.

In the legal system, knowledge is power and money is key. Set aside money and gather information now, before you or your husband file for divorce, so that you are in the driver's seat when it happens. Once the divorce is filed, everyone retreats to their separate corners, and it becomes much more difficult and costly to obtain the information and the money you need. The odds are high that, if your husband is anticipating divorce, he is already taking action to prevent you from accessing your money. I see this happen in virtually every divorce case I handle.

I had a client, Cecilia, who is a perfect case in point. Cecilia fell in love with Jeff, a handsome professional athlete, and they married when she was young. She became pregnant shortly after they married, and since Jeff traveled frequently with his team, she stayed home with first one baby, then two. When Jeff's career as a player ended, he became a coach for a professional sports team in Los Angeles. He made good money, and their family had a great life. Cecilia didn't have to work and devoted herself to raising the kids and enjoying the perks of being a coach's wife.

But then came the signs and the alarm bells — which Cecilia chose to ignore. Even after Jeff *left the home and was openly having an affair with another woman*, Cecilia believed that everything would be fine and that Jeff would "do the right thing." She remained in denial, hoping that Jeff would return to the family. Despite all the signs that her marriage was ending, Cecilia did nothing to prepare for the inevitable, until it all came to a screeching halt. One day, Cecilia and the kids arrived home from dinner while Jeff was traveling with the team. When they pulled into the garage, they found it empty. Their teenage son's Jeep was gone. They frantically called the police. Only after the police located Jeff, driving the Jeep, did the family realize what had happened: Jeff had returned early from the trip, loaded the Jeep with his belongings, cleaned out the joint checking account, and taken off. When Cecilia arrived at my office, she had $238 in her bank account. Jeff had taken over $300,000 from the joint account and transferred it to a separate account of his own — so she couldn't hire a lawyer.

In my work, Cecilia's story is not an isolated incident. Inevitably, as I unwind each woman's story, I find that financial infidelity often accompanies sexual infidelity. And virtually every woman is stunned to discover this. Don't let this happen to you. Take the following steps now to protect yourself and your children, and do not be naïve. Your husband may have pledged to look out for your best interests financially and otherwise during your marriage, but when your marriage is in trouble, it is up to you to arm yourself with money and information so that you have an edge. These are the first steps to take control of your future.

DIVORCE HACKS

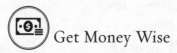 Get Money Wise

You will need funds to retain a lawyer and support yourself for several months until you can either negotiate support or obtain a court order. Take these steps to set aside the financial resources you need.

OPEN A BANK ACCOUNT IN YOUR NAME

Open this account at a *different* bank than the one where you and your husband share a joint account.

SET ASIDE MONEY FOR LIVING EXPENSES AND TO HIRE AN ATTORNEY

Did you know that you can take half the money out of your joint account and put it in a separate account in your own name if you live in one of the nine community-property states like California? You may not want to take out half the money all at once because it will alert your spouse to your intentions, and it may cause checks to bounce. At first, take out smaller amounts and put them in your new account, so that when the time comes, you can hire an attorney and cover your living costs for several months.

> **INSIDER TIP**
> *In community-property states, assets earned and acquired during the marriage are split 50/50. There are nine community-property states: Arizona, California, Idaho, Louisiana, Nevada, New Mexico, Texas, Washington, and Wisconsin.*

Secure your assets

During a divorce, I've seen valuable wine collections disappear, coin collections go missing, and money evaporate. Do not be surprised when your husband tells the judge that he has no idea what happened to the silver coins your grandfather left you — and the judge shrugs and moves on. Take steps now to protect what is yours; remove or hide valuable items. It is much easier to return items you have removed in order to protect them than it is to locate items someone else has spirited away.

Check your credit score

You need to build your own credit. Few numbers in life matter as much to your financial outlook and well-being as your credit score (known as the FICO score). A good credit score is crucial for financial success. It is one factor used by lenders to determine your creditworthiness for a mortgage, loan, or credit card. Your score can affect whether you are approved for credit and the interest rate you are charged. Prospective employers often check your credit score when you interview for a job. It is important to know what your credit score is and to improve it if it's not in the "good" range.

The three major credit-reporting agencies are Equifax, Experian, and TransUnion. You need to check your score with each agency because your score may differ between them. This is because some lenders report to all three credit agencies, but others do not. Since your credit report can contain errors that adversely affect your score, you need to check all three to make certain

> **Insider Tip**
> *Most states follow equitable distribution laws. In these states, property will be divided between the spouses in a fair and equitable manner. There is no set rule in determining who receives what or how much. The court considers a variety of factors. For example, the court may look at the relative earning contributions of the spouses, the value of one spouse staying at home or raising the children, and the earning potential of each. A spouse can receive between one-third and two-thirds of the marital property.*

that they are accurately reporting. Further, in 2017, Equifax suffered a major data breach, so if you have a credit report with them, check out the Federal Trade Commission's website for what to do.

You can easily access your score online for free and track your credit-building progress on sites such as CreditKarma.com or AnnualCreditReport.com. A "good" credit score is generally considered to be 720 or higher. Lenders, however, have different standards for what they consider to be a good credit score, and so it is important to keep building your score to receive the most favorable interest rates and the highest rates of credit approval. Later, I'll provide concrete tips for building your credit. For now, simply take the first step to find out what your credit score is.

Open two credit cards in your own name

You need to be the *primary cardholder* on at least two credit cards, if possible. You can have a wallet full of credit cards, but if your husband is the primary cardholder and you are the secondary, he can cancel those cards without your permission. So get at least two cards in *your name now*, while you can use your combined credit score to get approved. Once you are divorced, it may be harder to get credit in your own name if you don't have substantial income of your own.

Copy Financial Documents

When you meet with your attorney, he or she will ask for your financial documents. Save yourself time and money by collecting these documents now.

Gather and copy all financial documents, even those in your spouse's name

Copy anything with a dollar sign attached to it, such as bank accounts, investments, and retirement plans. Many women tell me their husband insists he is going to keep "his" 401K or pension. Wrong. If you live in a community-property state, half of any pension or retirement fund earned by your husband during the marriage is yours. If you live in an equitable property state, you are entitled to your fair share of his 401K or pension. Here is a checklist of documents your lawyer will want when you meet:

- **Employment information:** Paycheck stubs for you and your spouse for the last twelve months (or at least the last three months to the current date).
- **Tax returns:** Include the last three years of state and federal income tax returns.
- **Pension and retirement programs:** Copies of 401Ks, investment programs, stock, stock options, and bonds provided through the employer for you and/or your spouse.
- **Insurance:** Documents regarding insurance provided through the employer for you and/or your spouse.
- **Real property:** Deeds showing the legal description of any real property owned individually or jointly with your spouse, escrow papers from the time of purchase, current mortgage statements, current real property tax statements, homeowners or fire insurance policies on all real properties, and tax assessor's statements.
- **Stock portfolio:** List of corporate stocks and/or stock certificates owned by you and your spouse, individually or jointly, and the name and address of stock broker(s).
- **Cars, boats, trailers:** Copies of pink and registration slips, encumbrance (what's owed), and monthly payments.
- **Life insurance:** Current policies with statements of any loans against them.
- **Promissory notes and/or deeds of trust:** Copies of such records that name you and your spouse as beneficiaries.
- **Credit cards and loans:** Credit cards; creditor's statements showing names, address, account numbers, and

balances presently owed, plus creditor's statements showing balances *owed at separation date*; financial statements
of net worth prepared by you or your spouse to secure
bank loans or for any other purpose; and any other information that will help establish your net worth individually or jointly, for you and your spouse.

- **Household furniture and furnish-
  ings:** Take pictures of significant
  items with your opinion of the estimated value. You may be asked
  to list those items that you wish to
  keep and those that you wish to give
  to your spouse.

- **Bank or credit union accounts:** Most
  recent statements showing balances,
  particularly at date of separation,
  held in individual or joint names,
  savings passbooks, and certificates
  of deposit.

- **Wills or trusts**

- **Written agreements:** Premarital written agreements with spouse.

> **INSIDER TIP**
> *After filing for divorce,
> husbands often provide
> only a fraction of what they
> legally owe as a tactical
> maneuver to force their
> spouse to accept a settlement
> that is less than what she is
> legally entitled to. It can take
> time to retain counsel and
> get to court to obtain what
> you need. Take steps now to
> protect yourself.*

IF YOUR SPOUSE OWNS A BUSINESS, COPY FINANCIAL INFORMATION ABOUT THE BUSINESS

You must prove your husband's income to obtain support, and it is
more difficult to establish cash flow for a spouse who is self-employed
than one who receives a W-2. If your spouse is self-employed, he
will probably understate his earnings and overstate his business expenses to decrease what he owes in spousal and child support. Before the divorce is filed, obtain whatever information you can about
the business and its finances. Your lawyer will want the following:

- Corporate or partnership federal and state income tax returns for the past three years.
- Copies of recent financial statements prepared to apply for credit or business loans of any kind.

Document your monthly budget for household expenses

Gather information on all household expenses, for you and your children, including mortgage/rent, property taxes, homeowner's fees, car payment, insurance (home, car, medical, and life), utilities, personal expenditures, travel, education expenses, health care, and so on — everything, in other words, that you spend to maintain your standard of living on a monthly basis. This information will determine the amount of child and spousal support you will receive or pay. I recommend that for expenses that fluctuate (like the water and gas bill), you gather expenditures over the past twelve months and divide each category by twelve. It is important to include everything, since once support is ordered, getting it modified is costly and time-consuming, and can only be accomplished in certain circumstances. For example, if you do not include the expense for the children's summer camps in your calculation before the divorce is final, you may have difficulty getting your ex-husband to share that expense after the divorce.

 Know the Three Ways to Get Divorced

In order to get what you want in your divorce, it is imperative that you understand the different ways you can get divorced and select the best path for you. Understanding the pros and cons of each method will enable you to make an informed decision that will alleviate stress and save you time and money. There is a movement toward resolving divorce through mediation and collaboration, rather than litigation, which is generally a very good thing. However, if you take the mediation route, it is extremely important that you understand your rights, so that you get what you need and are legally entitled to. Many women enter mediation assuming their rights will be protected — but that is not the case if you are not represented by an attorney.

> **WISE WOMEN KNOW**
> *What you agree to in your divorce may be the most important financial decision of your life.*

Recently I received a call from a panicked woman with four young children who finalized her divorce through the mediation process. In doing so, she gave away many of her rights just to obtain "peace." Right after the divorce was finalized, she learned that her husband had had another child with his girlfriend *while the mediation was under way*! She was furious and wanted to "undo" the divorce. But sadly, it was too late.

Consider the following ways to get divorced and decide which makes the most sense for you.

Mediation

In mediation, you and your spouse meet with a mediator (usually an attorney or a retired judge) who will help you work toward settling the issues in your divorce — property division; division of debts; spousal support; and custody, visitation, and child support if you have children. Mediation is a voluntary process where the parties work with a *neutral* mediator to try to resolve their disputes without court hearings or a trial. Mediators help the parties work out voluntary agreements that promote individual and common interests through understanding and cooperation. Mediation is generally less contentious, less expensive, and sometimes less time-consuming than obtaining a divorce through the legal system.

However, not every divorce can be mediated. A couple of prerequisites must be met for mediation to work. First, both you and your spouse must be able to set aside your emotions and treat the divorce like the dissolution of a business partnership. And second, you both must be willing to cooperate and compromise. If there is too much acrimony or either of you are unable to work cooperatively toward a reasonable compromise, then mediation will not work. If one person is incapable of being reasonable or is using the process to stall or to vent their emotions, then mediation is a waste of time. Sometimes the parties must blow off some steam before they can mediate; therefore, the timing of when to engage in mediation is very important.

The mediator's neutrality means she or he does not represent either you or your spouse. The mediator is looking for ways for both parties to compromise, to meet in the middle, and if either person is unwilling, mediation will probably not work.

> **INSIDER TIP**
> *Even if you mediate, you should consider retaining an attorney to advise you along the way.*

Frequently, in divorces where the husband is the primary breadwinner, he is eager to mediate because he knows that if his spouse is not represented, he can wear her down through the negotiations. I am often sought out by husbands to advise them in advance of and during mediation to help them obtain what they want. Do not assume that the mediator is looking out for your best interests and that your husband is unrepresented. This can be a trap for the unwary.

Some mediators will have you and your spouse meet in the same room and work with you toward resolution. This process may be frustrating and nonproductive if you feel you cannot be in the same room as your spouse. As one client told me after dropping out of the mediation process, "If I could sit in a room with my husband and work things out, I wouldn't be getting divorced."

Mediation is completely voluntary. If the mediator makes recommendations that you do not agree with, you can stop the mediation and have an attorney represent you. Many couples try mediation because they assume it will be less costly and contentious, but for a variety of reasons, mediation can fail, and couples end up hiring attorneys to handle their divorce.

A common complaint is that the mediator is "ineffective" because she or he does not move the case along or push the other side to settle. Remember, the mediator is neutral and does not represent you or your spouse. Also, the mediator is looking for ways to get you and your spouse to compromise. Plus, since mediators do not go to court, if your spouse stalls as a tactic (which unfortunately happens often), there are no "teeth" to compel compliance or move things along. Many people find mediation to be frustrating, time-consuming, and expensive, and they end up hiring a lawyer when their divorce drags on indefinitely because their spouse refuses to settle and the mediator is powerless.

The Collaborative Approach

The collaborative approach involves a team approach where the parties agree to cooperate with one or more attorneys and advisers (such as accountants, appraisers, child-custody professionals, and therapists) to resolve their differences and develop positive communication skills for future contact. Through the collaborative process, the parties reach voluntary agreements on all of the issues in their case without court hearings or trial. This can minimize the impact of conflict on you and your children, and it provides greater support than mediation, since both you and your spouse are represented by attorneys and a team of other professionals during the process. If you and your spouse are able to work collaboratively, you can create personal solutions that are

> **INSIDER TIP**
> *You cannot use your collaborative attorney to go to court if the collaborative process fails. Collaborative attorneys sign an agreement that they will not go to court. If the collaborative process does not work out, you have to hire a new attorney. If your spouse is not a good candidate for collaboration, it could end up being more expensive to achieve your desired result.*

right for your family, maintain decision-making with you and your spouse, and preserve your privacy.

This approach is desirable if you have children, if you place a high priority on continued positive communication with your spouse following the divorce, and if the marital assets can be easily accounted for. However, it can be costly because there are more professionals involved, and if one spouse wants to drag things out or is unwilling to collaborate, your case can get bogged down, since there are no enforceable deadlines (unlike traditional litigation). If your spouse is untrustworthy and is not forthcoming regarding his income or assets, collaboration can be a trap.

If you do not have minor children or you prefer less contact with your spouse, then the added expense and effort of collaboration may not be worth it. Like mediation, the process is voluntary and nonbinding. So if you are unhappy at any point in the process, you can hire an attorney (who must be different from your collaborative attorney).

Like mediation, the collaborative process can be abused because the lawyers sign an agreement that they will not go to court. A husband who is hiding assets or minimizing income may use the collaborative process to his advantage. The lawyers cannot take discovery to uncover the hidden assets or establish a spouse's earning capacity and must rely upon whatever the parties voluntarily provide regarding their finances.

The following example illustrates the problems that can arise when one spouse is hiding assets and the parties are "collaborating." I was once asked to represent a wife, Charlene, when her collaborative case fell apart after *six years*. During this time, Charlene used much of her inherited savings to support herself and the children, while her husband, Richard, was transferring and hiding millions of dollars from the family businesses to offshore accounts. Throughout this period, Charlene and Richard were meeting regularly with their "collaborative" team of lawyers, accountants, and therapists, who were presumably helping them to arrive at an acceptable settlement while "keeping the peace." At the end of six years, when Charlene was about to run out of her inherited savings, Richard and his attorney tried to force her to accept a settlement that was a tiny fraction of what she was entitled to. Because they were in the "collaborative" process, Charlene's attorney could not take Richard's deposition or subpoena bank records to uncover the fraud. Charlene had to hire me and a new forensic accountant to get what she was entitled to.

Understand that the "collaborative" process is only as trustworthy as the people who are using it and that the lawyers are limited in what they can do to protect you because their hands are tied.

Traditional Litigation

Traditional litigation gets a bad rap for a variety of reasons. It can be costly, and litigation is uncertain. A virtual stranger — the judge — makes binding decisions on life-changing matters concerning you and your children. Sadly, the process can be abused by certain "professionals" who earn their living billing by the hour and who benefit by dragging out your case. Some take unnecessary actions to pad their bill.

However, many divorces are simply not amenable to mediation or the collaborative approach — if, for example, one of the parties suffers from a mental disorder or addiction, is completely unwilling to be reasonable, or is stalling as a tactic. In these cases, traditional litigation is the answer. If that applies to you, it is imperative that you find a skilled and trustworthy advocate to represent you.

A good divorce attorney will go to court only when necessary and will maneuver the case into settlement mode as soon as possible. Hiring a lawyer does not mean that you will go to trial, but you have that option available in the event your spouse is completely unreasonable. Court-imposed deadlines will also move your case along, which is particularly advantageous if your spouse is delaying on purpose or you are concerned that he is dissipating assets.

When I represent a client in traditional litigation, I am looking out for her best interests and simultaneously looking for an opportunity to move the case into settlement mode — often using a retired judge to act as a mediator. This approach blends the best attributes of mediation and collaboration, but affords my client strong representation and protection of her rights. If you go down the traditional litigation path, these are the attributes you want. Below and in chapter 2, I provide the secrets for finding a winning attorney.

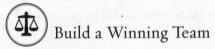 ## Build a Winning Team

Begin building your divorce team. Whether you mediate, collaborate, or go the traditional route, in most cases you will want to hire a good lawyer to advise you along the way. You will benefit from employing a team approach to your divorce. Think of it this way: When you married, you probably had a wedding planner, florist, caterer, hairdresser, DJ, and photographer. Your team made certain that everything came together according to your wishes on your wedding day.

Likewise, if you have assets and/or children, you will need a trusted team working together to obtain what you want. Your team may include an attorney, financial adviser, tax adviser (probably not the same adviser you currently use for your family), and therapist (for both you and your children). You do not need to get all these professionals on board immediately, but it is smart to begin taking steps to locate the right professionals.

The risks of *not* doing this right away are huge. I had a client, Patricia, who had been married for thirty-four years. Patricia, her husband, and their four children were the picture of the "perfect" family. Her husband was a successful businessman who was also a leader in their church. During their marriage, Patricia focused on raising the family and doing charitable work, while her husband built his multimillion-dollar real estate business. Their marriage began to crumble when the children left home for college and Patricia realized that she was unfulfilled.

Patricia trusted her husband to divide everything up fairly, so she didn't retain a lawyer. Because he was a devout church leader and had always handled the finances, she assumed that he would do the right thing and she would be taken care of. She ended up in my office after she signed a marital settlement agreement dividing the assets and setting spousal support, which her husband prepared. He convinced her to accept spousal support of $4,000 per month, terminating after ten years. She gave up her right to half his million-dollar pension, her interest in his business, and permanent spousal support of over $11,000 per month. In short, the churchgoing man she had been married to for over three decades and whom she trusted to look out for her best interests attempted to swindle her out of millions of dollars and her financial security. She finally realized, days before the judgment was entered, that she had given up her future financial security because she had trusted her husband. It took her months of energy and effort, not to mention tens of thousands of dollars in legal fees, to repair the damage and get what was due to her. Do not be naïve. Take steps to locate a good lawyer now.

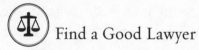 Find a Good Lawyer

Finding a good lawyer takes legwork. I suggest asking for referrals and then interviewing at least three divorce lawyers before deciding.

ASK YOUR DIVORCED FRIENDS FOR REFERRALS

An effective way to get information about the lawyers in your community is to ask divorced friends for referrals. Ask the following questions:

- How much did the attorney charge for a retainer (the amount to start the case), and how much did they

INSIDER TIP
Do not assume that because an attorney charges more or has a fancy office that he or she is a better attorney. Not necessarily so. They may only be better at taking your money!

charge per hour? You will know immediately whether you can afford to retain this lawyer. I am often asked how much it will cost to get divorced. It is impossible to quantify because it depends on how reasonable and how litigious the spouse is. But your lawyer can go to court and request that your husband pay your attorney's fees (and forensic accountant's fees) and costs. The court will insist upon evidence that your spouse has the resources to pay both his fees and yours before ordering him to do so. So keep these factors in mind when considering the expense of a lawyer.

- Did the lawyer return their calls and emails within twenty-four hours? You want a responsive attorney.

- How happy was your friend with the amount of support ordered and the division of assets? Happy clients are a good measure of an attorney's skill.

- How did the lawyer handle issues concerning children? Some lawyers are skilled in this area, and others are not.

- How often did the lawyer go to court and were they effective in obtaining the relief sought? The best attorneys will attempt to resolve issues without going to court and will use court as a last resort, but they will have the skills to obtain what is necessary if the other side is unreasonable.

- Did the lawyer do a good job preparing your friend for court appearances? Court appearances can be emotionally difficult, and you are often put on the spot around a variety of topics. A good lawyer helps clients know what might be coming and how to answer tough questions.

- Will the lawyer allow you to negotiate directly with your husband? Some lawyers will discourage this because they don't want the case to end. Timing is key here, but if your lawyer has done a good job setting the "guardrails" in the case (for example, had an early victory obtaining temporary support), sometimes a deal can be struck between the parties, without the lawyers' involvement.
- Did the lawyer send a monthly bill that was easy to understand and in the range anticipated? If not, how did the lawyer handle questions about the bill?
- Does the lawyer have a paralegal or assistant who will handle the clerical tasks at a lower rate than the attorney? This will decrease your legal bill, but still get the job done.
- How long did the divorce take? Most divorces can be finalized in a year or less. If all the attorney's cases take years to resolve, the lawyer may be dragging them out unnecessarily.

Ask your therapist for referrals

Therapists are an excellent resource for attorney referrals. Their clients often find themselves needing to get divorced, and many therapists will keep a referral list of lawyers and mediators. Usually they will refer you to someone who can be trusted to resolve matters when feasible, rather than ramping up the litigation to pad their bill.

Make appointments to interview three divorce lawyers

When making appointments, give yourself enough time to gather all the financial documents described above (or that the attorney requests). You want to bring these to review at the first meeting.

Consider Your Work Life

It can be frightening to face divorce and a potential reduction of income. Especially if you have been out of the workforce raising a family, so much will have changed that the idea of supporting yourself can be immobilizing. The way to deal with this is to 1) hire a good attorney who can get you the time and resources you need to create or obtain the job you want, and 2) consider your ability to earn in the new economy, which may be far greater than you think and provide needed flexibility. Even for my clients who have taken time off to raise their children, there are many opportunities available today to work from home, earn good money, and still be available to your kids. In the chapters that follow, I provide concrete steps to help you create work that meets your needs and suits your lifestyle, including starting your own business.

> **INSIDER TIP**
> *"Imputed income" is income that you are not earning but that a judge determines you are capable of earning. This is offset against any support you receive.*

Clients often ask whether they should delay working or quit their jobs to reduce their income during a divorce. Since both your and your spouse's incomes are used to calculate support, this is a valid concern. Strategy is important here. It is a mistake to assume that you will get adequate support from your husband to take care of you for the rest of your life in the manner to which you have become accustomed. Support is generally ordered in an amount and for a length of time that allows you to become self-supporting. If you do not work or are underemployed, and if you are healthy and able, the judge will likely order you to undergo a vocational examination to determine how much money you are capable of earning, and the judge will deduct that income from what you will get when making the support determination. Choosing not to work if you can work will probably backfire.

My own case illustrates how strategy matters when considering your work as you face divorce. I had worked as an attorney at a large corporate law firm, but I had taken several years off to raise our children. During the recession, my law firm dissolved, so going back to work there was not an option. However, I knew that if I didn't have a job when I went to court, the judge would impute the income that I could earn as a lawyer at a corporate firm and deduct that phantom income when determining how much support I would receive from my husband. Before heading to court, I began working as a legal writing teacher at one of the local law schools, and I earned a small income from that. I also took on contract work for a couple of local attorneys, which I could do remotely from home. This allowed me to be available to my children, while also getting back to work and brushing up on my skills. When the judge made the support determination, he used the income I was currently earning, which was far less than what I had earned as a corporate lawyer at a large law firm — and far less than what I knew I would go on to earn later. This strategy worked because I received more support than I would have received if I hadn't gone back to work. Most importantly, I was also on my way to earning what I needed in order to support myself and my children, which is the key to financial freedom and independence.

CONSIDER YOUR EDUCATION AND WORK HISTORY

The first step to your financial independence is to objectively evaluate the skills you developed in the past that you can use now to get back to work. Over the next months, you will obtain additional education or training if needed, work on your résumé, and build a network to find or create the right job. Right now, brainstorm about your skill set and how it matches up with the current work environment. Envision what you want to be doing five years from now so that you can get what you need to make that goal a reality.

MATCH YOUR SKILLS TO THE CURRENT LABOR MARKET

How can you apply your education and skills to today's labor market? There are so many opportunities to work remotely now. How can you use your skills to create a job for yourself that suits your current needs? For example, if you have school-age children, can you work from home so that you can be available to them when they arrive home from school? A client had taught school in Mexico before getting married and moving to the United States. She tutored local kids who needed help with Spanish and eventually grew her stay-at-home business into a successful enterprise employing several other tutors, whom she supervised. Another client worked in the health-care industry brokering insurance contracts for a large company. After she finalized her divorce, she set up her own online insurance brokering business using her skills and contacts. What can you create that will give you the income you need and the flexibility to live the life you want to live? Brainstorm now, and later chapters will provide specific steps and tools to turn that dream into a reality.

CONSIDER ADDITIONAL EDUCATION AND TRAINING

If you have been out of the workforce for a lengthy period, do you need education and/or training to bring your skills up-to-date? I had a client who had been a speech therapist for fifteen years before she stopped working to raise two children. She did some research and learned that it would take a year and approximately $3,500 for her to obtain the necessary certifications to begin working again as a speech therapist. We used that information to negotiate adequate support to give her the time and resources she needed to get back to work in a career that she was passionate about. Search your previous areas of expertise online to determine whether additional certifications and education are required to get back to work.

NETWORK TO MAKE CONNECTIONS

There is no substitute for networking. When you are getting back to work, it requires a certain vulnerability to let people know that you are looking, especially if you have been out of the workforce for a while — but the rewards are huge. Take the risk. My story is illustrative. I got divorced during a recession, and law firms were not hiring — they were firing. I knew that I would not be able to earn a living as I had in the past. I began making lunch and coffee dates with anyone I could think of who might have contacts in the legal community, so that I could get the word out that I wanted to get back to work. Through a series of those lunches and coffees, I was connected to the dean of a local law school. I expressed a desire to teach, something I hadn't done before. A few weeks later, on New Year's Day, the dean emailed me that one of the legal writing teachers was ill and couldn't teach that semester. He asked if I would step in. I did — one week before classes began. Although it was scary, I loved it. It took me out of my comfort zone, I learned I could do it, and I enjoyed being of service to the students — a win-win situation. You never know what opportunities are out there until you ask and show up. Take these steps now to get the word out that you are interested in getting back to work:

- Set up coffee or lunch with three friends to brainstorm about your skill set and explore what opportunities are available.
- End each meeting by asking each friend to recommend one other person you might speak with.
- Make sure to send thank-you notes or emails to people who meet with you and remind them to provide any other helpful contacts.
- On your computer or in a notebook, keep track of those you meet with and the outcome of each discussion. Use this document to add contacts, phone numbers, and

email addresses of anyone who may assist you as you build your network.

Recommended Resources for Finding Work You Love

- Richard Bolles, *What Color Is Your Parachute? 2018: A Practical Manual for Job-Hunters and Career-Changers* (Berkeley, CA: Ten Speed Press, 2017): This helpful manual shares proven tips for writing impressive résumés and cover letters, as well as guidance for effective networking, confident interviewing, and the best salary negotiating possible. But it goes beyond that by helping you to zero in on your ideal job — and guiding you toward fulfilling and prosperous work.
- Chris Guillebeau, *Born for This: How to Find the Work You Were Meant to Do* (New York: Crown Business, 2016): The intersection of joy, money, and flow is what Guillebeau will help you find in this book. Through inspiring stories of those who have successfully landed their dream career, as well as actionable tools, exercises, and thought experiments, he'll guide you through today's vast menu of career options to discover the work perfectly suited to your unique interests, skills, and experiences.
- Women for Hire (www.womenforhire.com): This site is geared to women returning to the workforce.
- PathSource (www.pathsource.com): Find a career, build a résumé, and post a job on this site.
- More (www.more.com/money/career-advice): A magazine roundup of career advice for women.
- DailyWorth (www.dailyworth.com): Financial advice geared to women.

Handling Issues Concerning Your Children

The greatest gift you can give your children now is your mindful awareness of how they are feeling. Children faced with divorce need to know that they are safe and loved, by both parents. Even if your husband is a louse, do not bad-mouth him in front of your children. It will backfire. And do not use your children as therapists, even if they seem capable of listening and giving good advice. That is what a therapist is for. Let your children be children, while you attend to grown-up tasks.

> **WISE WOMEN KNOW**
> *You are only as happy as your least-happy child.*

DOCUMENT ANY INSTANCES OF ABUSE

Judges consider domestic violence (against you or your children) when making custody orders. Keep a diary of any instances of physical, verbal, or emotional abuse of you or your children with specific reference to dates, times, places, and details of what happened. In the legal system, specificity is required to prove your case. General allegations of abuse will not meet the legal standard. Your lawyer will ask you to keep a written record if abuse is an issue in your case, so start now.

MAXIMIZE YOUR TIME WITH YOUR CHILDREN

Maximize your time with your children as you prepare for divorce. This is not only the right thing to do, it is the *smart* thing to do. Judges tend to enforce the status quo when making orders concerning custody and visitation and when ordering parenting plans, which means a judge is likely to maintain the parenting routine that is in place, absent abuse. So, *before* you file for divorce, implement the plan you want ordered. I had a client who changed her work

INSIDER TIP
Dads often insist on more time with the kids when divorce is imminent. Why? Usually because the more time he spends with the kids, the less he will pay in child support. Set your desired time with the kids before you file for divorce, since most judges enforce the status quo.

schedule to allow her to work from home several days a week and spend more time with her five-year-old daughter. When the judge ordered the parenting plan, my client benefited greatly from the changes to her schedule that she implemented before filing for divorce.

It's not necessary to explain to your boss that you are requesting the adjustment to your schedule because you are divorcing; rather, tell your boss that you will be more productive if you work from home on certain days. In today's workplace, it is common to telecommute, and it is understood that it can increase productivity, particularly for parents of school-age children. Most employers recognize that telecommuting boosts productivity, performance, job satisfaction, and overall life satisfaction. You can use this to your advantage as you set the "status quo" and manage your work/life balance.

 Consider Your Living Situation

If you are considering moving out of your home before filing for divorce, consult with an attorney first, since this can have significant financial implications and affect custody. Moving out constitutes the "date of separation" in many but not all states. The date of separation is typically defined as when spouses have come to a parting of the ways with no intention to continue the marriage. Although states vary as to how they define date of separation, the couple's conduct must evidence a complete and final break in the marriage.

Up until the date of separation, a spouse may be entitled to the property acquired or share the debt incurred by the other spouse. The following example illustrates the importance of understanding the date of separation and how it can affect your finances. Mary's husband was about to receive a multimillion-dollar bonus. After thirty-three years of marriage, he tapped her on the shoulder one morning and told her he was moving out. He received the bonus the next day. His lawyer claimed that because he had moved out, the bonus was his separate property. However, because he *earned* it before he moved out, Mary was entitled to half of it.

The date of separation can determine when a spouse becomes responsible for child support and spousal support. For example, if a husband who earns all the household income moves out of the marital residence, a court can order him to pay temporary child support and alimony from the date he left. In some states, however, a spouse may only be eligible for child support or alimony after filing for divorce and asking for support.

Moving can also impact your custody rights. If you have young children and move out of the family home, it may be more difficult to get the parenting plan you want. Some judges tend to rule in favor of keeping the children in the family home with the parent who resides there, while the "out" parent gets visitation.

> **INSIDER TIP**
> *If you want to keep the house after the divorce, you may want to consider refinancing to lower the mortgage payment, and if so, consider doing this* before *the divorce is finalized so that you can use your husband's credit history, if it is good. He may agree to do this so that you and the children can remain in the family home.*

 Learn the Fair Market Value of Your Home

You do not have to decide whether to keep or sell the family home right away. Whew! But your lawyer will ask for information to help you assess whether it makes sense to keep or sell the home. Familiarize yourself with the fair market value of your home, the amount of equity in the home, the monthly mortgage payment, and whether there is a home equity line of credit (HELOC) or a second mortgage on the home. If you do eventually decide to sell your home, you will want to get a formal appraisal (see "Get Appraised," page 186), but you don't need one at this point.

Go to Zillow.com to quickly estimate the fair market value of your home

It's easy to find out approximately what your home is worth on Zillow.com. While not as accurate as a formal appraisal, it is a quick-and-easy way to get an approximation of your home's value. And it's free!

Calculate the estimated equity in your home

Look at the last mortgage statement to see what is owed on the home. Subtract this from the home's value on Zillow to obtain a rough estimate of equity.

Figure the estimated monthly payments

The mortgage statement will provide the monthly mortgage payment. Add to this the HELOC or second mortgage payment to come up with the total monthly payment for the house. You will need this information to determine whether you can continue to make those payments if you keep the house or whether it makes sense to sell.

 Create a Mindfulness Practice

Even if your husband is not on the path to enlightenment, *you* can be conscious as you uncouple. Mindfulness during this time is essential. Whether you have decided to end your marriage or your husband has pulled the trigger, you are undoubtedly experiencing deep feelings of loss, anger, anxiety, and fear about the future. These negative emotions can come and go without warning — causing you to panic or shut down.

A daily mindfulness practice will ground you so that you can deal with what needs to be dealt with and not be overcome or derailed by strong, negative emotions. It will allow you to be present with whatever is happening, no matter what it is.

In my case, my mindfulness practice literally saved my life as I presided over the demise of my marriage. Losing my husband was just the tip of the iceberg. The financial repercussions were devastating. It was the height of the 2008–2009 financial crisis, and both of our legal careers took a hit. We lost everything — our home, our car, our way of life. And shortly after we separated, my father, who was "my rock," passed away.

> WISE WOMEN KNOW
> *"Life is 10 percent what happens to you and 90 percent how you react to it."*
> — Charles R. Swindoll

My previous coping strategies, like going to the gym to work off stress, were inadequate to deal with the loss of everything I had held dear and the uncertain future we faced. I was literally brought to my knees by the catastrophic end of everything I had known.

Truly humbled by the experience, I acknowledged that this was bigger than me and that I needed a radical new approach. My mental problem-solving strategies weren't enough. I hit my knees and asked for help — and as I surrendered and acknowledged that I needed help, help arrived. Sometimes not the way I expected, like the time my neighbor's father asked me to trim the large tree that was overhanging the fence into his daughter's yard. Since we were moving, I was reluctant to spend money trimming that enormous ficus. But I did, and then he offered to rent one of his houses to me, at precisely the moment I needed to find a new place to live and at a price I could afford.

How exactly did I get the help I needed?

- **Meditation and prayer:** Each morning before the kids woke up, I would spend at least fifteen minutes sitting cross-legged on the floor, taking deep breaths and

quieting my mind. I would then ask for help and guidance from my "Higher Power" so that I could let go of
what needed to be let go, allow life to unfold, and make
good decisions that day. Your Higher Power may be
God or the universe or another power; it doesn't matter. Admitting you need help and asking for it is all that
is required.

- **Reading the masters:** I incorporated spiritual and uplifting reading into my morning routine, which grounded
me for the challenges of the day ahead.
- **Journaling:** I began writing in a journal about my deepest fears, which allowed me to see that as life unfolded,
most of my fears were unfounded.

I found that these three things, practiced each day, allowed me
to let go of my feelings of anger and fear and instead focus with
gratitude on the things that mattered — the love of my children,
our health, and how I showed up in the present moment. As I experienced the benefits of this practice, I increased the time spent med-
itating, asking for guidance, writing in my journal, and pondering
what I read. And as I expanded my mindfulness practice into all aspects of my life, the results were profound and impactful. My ability
to handle the unexpected increased exponentially. In the following
chapters, I outline specific steps you, too, can take to radically trans-
form your life for the better.

Action Steps to Mindfulness

To accomplish what I describe above, practice the following action
steps:

- Create a place in your home for meditation. This should
be a quiet place, like your bedroom, where you can rest
from stress, pray, and write in a journal. You might
create an altar and put pictures or tokens on it of the
things in life that bring you joy. My altar is a Buddha,

and over time, I have added pictures and mementos from my children, parents, and others that have had a positive impact on my life. When I sit before it in silence, it calms and centers me.

- Set aside time each day for meditation. Start each day quietly before your altar, close your eyes, and take long, slow, deep breaths. Each time a thought enters your mind, acknowledge it and return your focus to your breathing. Begin with just a few minutes each day, and gradually increase the time spent in mindful meditation. Don't worry if you don't know how to meditate or don't know what to do. Just sit with yourself and pay attention to your breath. You will become aware of the constant worry and chatter that infiltrates your mind. As you become aware of this, practice being the observer. Simply observe the chatter and redirect your attention to your breath. You will find that if you stick with this practice, you will begin to experience more ease and calm.

- After quieting your mind, ask for help from whatever source you believe in (God, the universe, a Higher Power). Ask for assistance with whatever might arise during the day. Just simply acknowledge that you need help and ask for it.

- Start a journal. After spending time in silent meditation, write whatever comes to mind in your journal. Don't edit what comes out. Just write it out. This stream-of-consciousness writing will allow you to get any negative, repetitive thoughts out of your head and onto the page. It will free your mind so that you aren't stuck ruminating on things over which you have no control. This will allow you to see, as time goes on, that many of your worst fears are unfounded.

- Read for at least ten minutes from the books listed

below and commit to practicing the truths they reveal. As you engage in this practice, record its impact in your journal. Your life will change and it will be better.

Recommended Reading for Supporting Mindfulness

- Tara Brach, *Radical Acceptance: Embracing Your Life with the Heart of a Buddha* (New York: Bantam, 2004): A psychotherapist and Buddhist meditation teacher, Brach interweaves stories from her own life as a hardworking single mother with anecdotes from her therapy practice, and she offers examples of how our pain can become a doorway to love and liberation.
- Marianne Williamson, *Illuminata: A Return to Prayer* (New York: Riverhead Books, 1995): Prayer is practical, according to Williamson. It can deliver us from deep psychic pain and provide peace and understanding. *Illuminata* shows you how to bring prayer into your daily life.
- Deepak Chopra, *The Seven Spiritual Laws of Success: A Practical Guide to the Fulfillment of Your Dreams* (Novato, CA: New World Library, 1994): Deepak Chopra distills the essence of his teachings into seven simple yet powerful principles that can be applied to all areas of your life. This book will inspire you to understand that all is possible. Uncertainty is our friend. Limitless opportunity awaits.

CHAPTER 2

Taking Action

"Action is the antidote to despair."

— Joan Baez

*T*here are two big challenges to leaving a soul-deadening re-lationship: the difficulty of stepping out of your comfort zone and the fear of the unknown. Even if miserable, many women stay in a loveless marriage because they prefer what they know over the uncertainty of what they don't know. This is human nature, but you do not have to be stuck and wait for a crisis to create positive change.

First, simply acknowledge that change can feel threatening. Neuroscientists call this fundamental principle the "walk toward, run away" theory. We are biologically wired to avoid what seems threatening, rather than embrace it. If we feel uncertain, we focus on the negative and disengage. As a result, our prefrontal cortex, which is the area of the brain engaged for changing behavior and habits, has less reserves of energy (oxygen and glucose) so we are less likely to make good decisions, take on new ideas, and appreciate the big picture. In other words, because of the way our brains are wired, it is harder for us to break out of familiar bad patterns than it is to try something new. This is why most women avoid filing for divorce until calamity strikes.

Next, understand that the way through the fear of change brought on by divorce is to have a strong mindfulness practice and a strategic, step-by-step plan. The mindfulness practice prepares you for the changes you will face. The practical plan provides the steps to get you through it. Dissolving a marriage sounds messy, complicated, and frightening, but it doesn't have to be. I know you can do what you need to do to establish a new life because I see women accomplish this every day, and they are no different than you. Have courage and move forward to a new and better life.

> WISE WOMEN KNOW
> *"When one door closes, another opens; but we often look so long and so regretfully upon the closed door that we do not see the one which has opened for us."*
> — Alexander Graham Bell

DIVORCE HACKS

Facing the Truth of Infidelity

In virtually every divorce case I handle, one of the spouses is cheating on the other. Sometimes the woman is doing the cheating, but more often than not, it's the man. And when there is cheating, there is often "financial infidelity" — marital funds spent on unauthorized activity. It is an inconvenient truth, and we tend to think that we are immune — until it happens to us.

A male client, a well-respected "family man," told me something that every woman considering divorce should know. He had been carrying on an affair for quite some time without his wife's knowledge. He said, in the most matter-of-fact way, "This is what we do." What he meant was that, when the going gets tough, men will use sex like they would use a shot of tequila — to distract themselves from the stresses of modern life. Whether it's internet porn, strip clubs, or actual hookups, the truth is, many men routinely engage in sex outside of marriage, particularly when they are experiencing stress.

In today's world, modern technology makes access to willing partners more available and lowers inhibitions, creating a perfect storm for men looking for sexual relief. Recent studies reveal that, not surprisingly, Facebook and Twitter users have a higher rate of infidelity and divorce. There are 40 million sexually explicit websites, chat rooms, bulletin boards, and interactive games available on the internet. An estimated 20 to 33 percent of internet users go online for sexual purposes; most are male, about thirty-five years old, married with children, and well-educated. Online sexual behavior is proving to be highly addictive to some users, and serious relationship problems are reported in almost all marriages in which one partner is cybersex addicted. As many as 17 percent of internet users become addicted to online sexual activity.

> **WISE WOMEN KNOW**
> *"Life is like riding a bicycle. To keep your balance, you must keep moving."*
> — Albert Einstein

Many women think they can change their spouse, or that a marital counselor, therapist, or religious adviser will bring him around and get him to cease his extramarital sexual activities. Having been taught to be patient and "carry on," women often wait for their husbands to come around. But there is a very real and present danger to waiting. The following story illustrates this point.

Rebecca's husband, John, had lost his high-paying corporate job in finance during the 2008 financial crisis. Rebecca's parents were wealthy, and so they loaned Rebecca and John money so that they wouldn't lose their luxurious beachside home in Los Angeles. Rebecca's parents also paid for their three grandchildren to go to elite private schools and for Rebecca and John to regularly vacation in Hawaii and Aspen. They paid for their membership in several country clubs and for John's Audi and Rebecca's Lexus. This was a great gig for John. He spent a lot of time playing tennis at the country club.

After a few years of this, Rebecca came to me because the financial crisis was over, and although John was highly qualified to obtain a job, he hadn't gone back to work. She had also learned that John was having an affair. Under these circumstances, Rebecca's parents were refusing to continue to pay the bills, and Rebecca wanted to know what she could do to bring John back. She and John were in counseling with the pastor of their church. John said that he wanted to "do the right thing," but despite his promises, she knew (from accessing his text messages) that he was still carrying on the affair. I suspected that what John really wanted was for the gravy train to continue, and I recommended that Rebecca file for divorce. She didn't. Instead, over the next six months, Rebecca nagged, cajoled, and threatened John — but nothing changed — until one night, the girlfriend came to Rebecca's house and threatened Rebecca in an effort to extort money. It took a dramatic moment, but Rebecca finally realized that her marriage was over.

Do not be Rebecca. Don't wait for someone to hit you over the head with bad news. If your husband is not taking active steps to change unacceptable behavior, then it's up to you to take action. It could literally save your life.

When It's Time to Admit the Marriage Is Over

Among the women who come through the door of my legal practice, I often observe a great deal of "magical thinking." The woman is depleted and confused and unsure whether to get divorced. She knows something is wrong — her husband isn't "showing up fully" and finances have become strained — but she doesn't have a complete picture of what is happening. Often, by the time she sees me, the woman is already in marital counseling with her husband, who continues to proclaim that he wants to "do the right thing." While at first this placated her to a certain degree, nothing has changed, and so she asks me — a divorce attorney — what she should do.

Typically, women don't come to me already convinced that they want to untie the knot of their marriage. They want reassurance that they don't need to do anything — yet. Sometimes, a woman will decide to file for divorce as a "wake-up call," hoping this will bring her husband to his senses and she won't have to follow through. Women often hope against hope to save their marriages, even when, from the outside, it's easy to see they are already broken beyond repair. In-stead, the woman dances around the truth for a while, until one day, I receive an emergency phone call — often on Saturday morning, usually very early. The woman has just learned that her husband has been carrying on a lengthy affair. She usually finds out because he is careless with his cell phone or computer or someone posts some-thing on social media. The woman is *always* shocked — first by the infidelity, and then, as we unwind the tangled web of her life, by other revelations. We often learn that, in addition to his infidelity, her husband has been draining marital assets to support his "secret life."

> WISE WOMEN KNOW
> *"All great changes are preceded by chaos."*
> — Deepak Chopra

Even in the face of duplicity and betrayal, many women still refuse to acknowledge that the marriage is over, and they wait to take action, still hoping for their husband to come to his senses. A woman will sometimes convince herself that her husband is just going through a phase and will come back around. I am here to tell you that it rarely happens, and the inability to face the truth often leads to financial and emotional ruin for the woman.

Admitting that your marriage is over and taking appropriate action is often the hardest choice to make. I know, from personal experience and from working with my clients, how hard it is. It re-quires tremendous courage to take the first step out of your mar-riage and into a new life. No one can make the decision to get a divorce for you. But if you have lost your sense of joy, life has become a struggle, and the red flags are flying, it is time to wake up and take action.

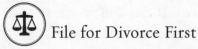 File for Divorce First

Once you've decided to end your marriage, take control of your life and file for divorce first. Doing so, you will set the agenda, the pace, and the tone of your divorce, and you will take charge of your future. Do not delay. Before your husband is served with papers, he can move assets and money with few repercussions — and it happens all the time. Once he is served, he can no longer move or dissipate assets. Take control of the process, hire a lawyer, and move forward.

In my work, I see many women who are taken advantage of because they are hesitant to take the first step. Whether women are in denial or clinging to hope that the marriage can be saved — delaying is a recipe for disaster. Consider Sara's story. Sara sensed there were problems in her marriage, and she convinced her husband to attend counseling, which they did for several years. Her husband claimed that he also wanted to save their marriage, but during this time, he bought a Porsche, got plastic surgery on his face, traveled out of the country frequently "on business," and claimed that his income from self-employment was radically reduced, despite the good economy. He eventually told Sara that he wanted a divorce and convinced her to attend mediation. After it became clear that her husband was using mediation in an attempt to minimize what he was going to pay her in spousal support, Sara hired me. After our first meeting, I discovered (through social media) that Sara's husband was having an affair with a woman in Brazil who claimed to be his "wife" and that he was draining funds from their business to pay for his international trips to visit his girlfriend. He was also claiming these trips as business expenses. In other words, Sara's hesitation gave her husband all the time he needed to enjoy his dalliance, drain their bank account, and subject Sara to possible tax liability for claiming business expenses illegally. He'd set things up to take full advantage of Sara.

I sometimes find it hard to believe the lengths men will go in their efforts to minimize their support obligations to their wives and children, but they can get very crafty. One such case was the story of the "soiled woman." Catherine and Bill lived in California, had been married for twenty years, and were in marriage counseling because Bill had had multiple affairs. During counseling, Catherine admitted that she had also had a brief "fling" during the marriage. Although Catherine knew that the marriage needed to end, she was dragging her feet. She had never worked and was reluctant to file for divorce because of the financial support Bill provided, since he was a successful businessman. Meanwhile, Bill filed for divorce in Idaho, where he had established residency after living there only six weeks. Since Idaho is a "fault" state, the judge found that Catherine's affair caused her to be a "soiled woman"; therefore, he ruled that she was not entitled to spousal support. Had Catherine filed first in California, she would have been entitled to significant spousal support under California law, which is a "no fault" state.

Once you've decided that your marriage is over, do not delay. Make the first move. This is an essential step to taking back your power.

 Regain Control If Your Husband Filed First

If your husband files for divorce first, do not fear. Inevitably, this will be a surprise, but you can handle the unexpected and take control. Remember my client Mary from chapter 1? The morning when her husband of thirty-three years, Mark, tapped her on the shoulder and said, "I'm leaving," Mary assumed Mark was going to the gym or maybe to pick up bagels for breakfast. He was dressed in his workout clothes. So Mary turned back to her computer to keep working. Then Mark said, "You need to retain a lawyer."

When Mary walked through the doors of my office, she was still shocked and surprised. As she described it to me, after their youngest child had headed off to college, she and Mark had grown apart, and they were in marital counseling. Mark had recently been fired from his high-paying job as the CFO of a bank, and he was depressed. Mary felt certain that they would get back on an even keel — and then, that Saturday morning.

After further investigation, the facts turned out to be quite different. Instead, Mark had been carrying on a lengthy affair with a colleague at the bank, and he had retired early from his high-paying job so that he could travel around the world with his girlfriend. When he tapped Mary on the shoulder, it was the day before he was to receive a million-dollar payout on his deferred compensation plan. Mark had filed for divorce without telling Mary in an effort to avoid providing her with her fair share of this deferred compensation.

Although Mary was surprised by Mark's actions, she did the right thing. Rather than spend months licking her emotional wounds, she immediately retained counsel. Doing so saved her financially. We were able to uncover Mark's real motives, which were to start a new life with his girlfriend and shirk his obligations to his family. By taking quick and decisive action, Mary secured what she needed financially for herself and her children.

No matter what your circumstances, if your spouse's desire for divorce takes you by surprise, you will probably feel as if the bottom has dropped out from under you. You will need time to calm your raw emotions, restore your self-esteem, and start to heal. You should not, however, wait to protect your legal rights, financial assets, and access to your children. Even if the pain is so enormous that you can hardly think, hire a lawyer and follow the advice below to shore up your strategic position.

HIRE A LAWYER

The second you're told you will be involved in divorce, hire a lawyer. For help with this, see below, "Retain Counsel but Arm Yourself with Knowledge," and in chapter 1, "Find a Good Lawyer" (page 15). Be sure to tell your lawyer about any problems that might require relief from the court: the need for money for yourself or your children; the need to decide, at least on a temporary basis, where the children will live and what the visitation arrangements will be; and in some cases, the need for protection from your spouse.

PROTECT YOUR RIGHTS AS A PARENT

If you are a parent, the most important thing to do is to consult your lawyer to make sure that you are doing everything possible to protect your rights with regard to your children.

NEVER ACT OUT IN REVENGE

You must also avoid trampling on the rights of your husband, no matter how you feel about him. You may be furious, but don't act in ways you might regret later, such as locking your spouse out of the house or abandoning your marital residence with or without the children. If you do so, you stand to damage your position regarding custody and assets. If you leave the house, the judge could order that your husband remain in the residence — with the kids — until things are settled. If you lock your spouse out, the judge could order you to let him

---

INSIDER TIP

Heather was so furious at Steve for divorcing her that she hacked into his email, sent threatening messages to his girlfriend, and sent embarrassing emails to his family, friends, and coworkers. Heather felt this was acceptable because "all is fair in love and war." But at trial, her actions merely enraged the judge, who found that Heather had broken the law with her spying and threats. The judge's discretionary decisions were made in favor of Steve. Keep your anger in check. Angry or aggressive acts can be used against you once the legal system is involved.

back in. Resist any urge to engage in "revenge spending." It might be used against you later if your case goes to court.

GATHER INFORMATION

You must protect yourself against any preemptive moves your spouse may have taken without your knowledge. Directly ask your spouse for any papers that are suddenly missing. Make sure that the safe deposit box or family safe has not been raided, and if it has, you will need to immediately notify your attorney. With your lawyer's help, you can get restraining orders against the use of specific bank accounts.

TAKE CHARGE OF YOUR FINANCES

If your husband has filed or asked for a divorce, you will need to protect your financial position by learning all you can about your family's finances. Follow the tips in "Get Money Wise" (page 3) and copy all relevant financial documents. Then make some financial moves of your own. If your spouse hasn't yet raided the bank accounts, withdraw half of the savings accounts and open a new account. Do not spend that money if at all possible because you may need it until you can obtain relief through the legal system.

WHAT TO DO ABOUT CREDIT CARDS

If you share credit cards that are in your name, or if you pay the credit card bills, cancel them. Tell your husband you've canceled the cards. Since he has announced plans to divorce, this should not come as a surprise. On the other hand, if you have not yet established credit in your own name, now is the time to do so; use your spouse's credit lines to build some credit of your own. Obtain and complete applications immediately. For more, see "Establish and Build Your Credit" below.

WHERE TO SLEEP

If the two of you are going to live together until the divorce is final, decide where you'll sleep. Note that because your spouse told you that he wants the divorce, you can probably successfully demand use of the bedroom, since he may be feeling some guilt.

TAKE CARE OF YOUR CHILDREN

If you and your spouse can still have a civil conversation, decide how and what the two of you will tell the children about the divorce; for more on this, see "How and When to Tell Children You Are Divorcing" (page 54). If things are not civil, don't deliberately or inadvertently allow children to become involved. Do not put children in a loyalty bind, where they feel they must choose sides or parents.

CONSIDER SEEING A THERAPIST

There are going to be many stresses in the future, emotional as well as financial, and the better you can cope with them, the smoother the divorce process will go for you. See "Seek Help" at the end of this chapter to help find a therapist.

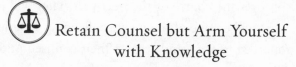

Retain Counsel but Arm Yourself with Knowledge

There are several things you can do during your first meeting with an attorney to reduce the pain, conflict, and cost of your divorce. Understanding these issues can help you overcome the obstacles that make divorce more difficult than it needs to be.

You, not a lawyer, should be in control of your divorce. Here's how: Arm yourself with knowledge and information. In chapter 1, "Get Money Wise" (page 3) outlines the financial documents that you will need to get divorced. Bring them to your first meeting. Your lawyer bills by the hour. From the very first meeting, use the time wisely. The worst approach is to go see a lawyer and just ask for a divorce without any information or preparation. In essence, you are asking the lawyer to take charge of your divorce — and your life — and it may not matter to the lawyer if your case becomes some sort of uncontrolled battle that leads to uncontrolled legal fees. That's great for the lawyer's bank account. The only way to protect yourself is to take control of your divorce.

Have a list of questions. Be specific and focused. Do not use your lawyer as a therapist. Nothing runs up the legal bill faster than a client who spends time venting their emotions. Vent about your ex with a friend or with a therapist, who charges much less. Do not send your attorney every email and text between you and your spouse. Your lawyer will charge you for the time spent reading these, and most of them will probably be redundant.

> INSIDER TIP
> *Before every meeting or phone call with your attorney, repeat this mantra, "My lawyer bills by the hour." Make every minute matter.*

Interview three lawyers. And before the interview, ask whether you will be charged for the initial consultation. Some attorneys charge for the initial meeting, others do not. Ask the questions outlined below. Then — consult your gut. You will be working closely with this person over the course of the next year. They will guide you through what will be one of the most challenging experiences of your life. You need to trust and respect their counsel. And you need to get along. If you connect with your lawyer and use your time to ask prepared, thoughtful questions, they will answer your phone calls and emails sooner and listen to you and what you want. You want a lawyer who is honest and direct — who can tell you when what you want can be accomplished and when it can't, and provide solutions to seemingly intractable problems. You want a lawyer who won't stir up conflict to create unnecessary work to pad their bill. In short, you want a lawyer who is looking out for your best interests.

QUESTIONS TO ASK THE LAWYER

- *How many years have you practiced family law?* Many lawyers claim to be family law lawyers, but they do not have much actual experience practicing in this area. Experience is key.

- *How many divorces have you handled?* You want a lawyer who has a track record handling divorces.
- *What is the average length of time between filing for divorce and resolution? How long does your average case take?* Most cases should be resolved within a year.
- *What percentage of your cases go to trial?* This should be a small number.
- *How many cases have you tried?* You want a lawyer who knows what they are doing in a courtroom, but not one that tries every case. Most cases should settle.
- *How much do you charge per hour?* Find out the going rate in your area by inquiring through the interview process and asking your divorced friends. Remember that just because a lawyer charges more does not mean that they are better.
- *What is your retainer?* This is the deposit the lawyer will require to begin work on your case. Again, find out what the going retainer is where you live. Some lawyers will split it in half to begin work on your case. Ask.
- *When will I receive an invoice and how do you handle billing disputes?* You should receive an invoice each month that clearly explains each task and the time spent. Questions about the bill should be handled immediately.
- *Can I pay by credit card?* Some lawyers won't do this because the credit card companies charge a fee, which is a deduction from what the lawyer receives. But it is a convenience and sometimes a necessity for clients.
- *When do you recommend using formal discovery?* That is, depositions, requests for production of documents, interrogatories, and so on. Formal discovery is rarely needed in family law because the parties are required to turn everything over in their financial disclosures.

However, many lawyers like to take unnecessary discovery to pad their bill. Be wary of this one!

- *Will I need a forensic accountant, and if so, who do you recommend?* If separate funds were used toward the acquisition of property that you and your spouse own jointly, you will probably need a forensic accountant to trace those funds. If you or your spouse own a business, you may need a forensic accountant to conduct an income analysis. Find out which forensics the attorney works with and ask to meet for a consultation (see "How a Forensic Accountant Can Help," page 176).

 ## When to Hire a Divorce Financial Planner

You may be asking yourself whether you *really* need a financial adviser if you're hiring a divorce lawyer. Quite frankly, it depends on the size and number of your assets. In simple, straightforward divorces, where the parties have few assets, you do not need a financial adviser. However, if you have significant assets that will be divided in the divorce and that you will then manage, you will want to enlist the help of a certified divorce financial planner. A divorce financial planner can work with you and your attorney to negotiate a divorce settlement that fully addresses your immediate financial needs as well as to avoid long-term financial pitfalls due to poor choices or financial ignorance.

Divorce financial planners can help with the following:

- Create a realistic budget as you move through the divorce process and beyond.
- Educate you on the financial characteristics of your assets, such as tax implications.
- Determine a long-term financial plan for your life as a single adult.

Working with you and your family law attorney, a divorce financial planner can forecast the long-term effects of various divorce settlement options, including tax liabilities and benefits; develop detailed household budgets to avoid postdivorce financial struggles; and help you think through what your divorce will realistically cost in the long run.

Hire a Certified Financial Planner

There is a significant difference between a "financial planner," a "divorce financial planner," and a "Certified Financial Planner" (CFP), which is a licensed certification. You want to find a Certified Financial Planner who is also a Certified Divorce Financial Analyst (CDFA).

The only people who call themselves "financial planners" are those who are not licensed. It is a generic term. Often, it means the "financial planner" is able to sell insurance, and that's all. Becoming a Certified Financial Planner requires a bachelor's degree, plus specialized curriculum that takes eighteen months to two years to complete. Candidates currently sit for a seven-hour comprehensive test. A CDFA is licensed by the Institute for Divorce Financial Analysts (IDFA), has additional training, is expert in the financial aspects of the divorce code in their state, and is subject to oversight. Divorce financial planning is a process, not a product. It focuses on a specific life transition encompassing the divorce and life afterward.

Often "divorce planners" will offer their services to do financial planning, but with strings attached: For example, you may agree to engage them later to manage any investments (brokerage accounts, 401Ks) or proceeds you might receive postdivorce. *Such an arrangement might create a conflict of interest.* This might result in the adviser designing the outcome so there are assets to manage, as opposed to the best result for a client (for example, keeping your house). Focusing solely on the divorce process, rather than on the potential of asset management, avoids this conflict.

Divorce financial planning is not forensic accounting, which investigates the past and is used to determine the value of assets, such as a business or other investments. It's a forward-looking process that focuses on lifestyle issues relevant to divorce: For example, divorce financial planners consider respective postseparation financial needs; the paying abilities of the parties; division of assets; and the financial workability of potential outcomes.

Anyone can call themselves anything, but it's worth your time and safety to understand the level of professionals who are on your team. Your divorce attorney undergoes continuing legal education to maintain his or her license. Likewise, you want a divorce financial planner who does, too.

QUESTIONS TO ASK BEFORE HIRING A DIVORCE FINANCIAL ADVISER

- *When did you receive your certification as a CFP, CDFA, or CPA?* This is an indicator of experience.
- *Do you have a specific background in taxation or accounting?* You definitely want your financial planner to understand the tax implications of dividing your assets. This can make an enormous difference in the decision-making and planning process.
- *How many divorce cases have you completed?* Another indicator of experience.
- *Do you have experience in complex property divisions, and if so, will you illustrate multiple scenarios?* Many divorce financial planners have software available that allows them to run various property-division scenarios, which can be used to evaluate the best approach for negotiating division of assets during divorce.
- *Are you familiar with calculations regarding employee stock options, restricted stock, and/or executive compensation?* This is critical if these assets are at issue in your divorce.
- *Can I see a sample of the written divorce financial plan you provide to your clients?* If the planner is qualified, they should be able to provide you with exemplars of the work they have done in this area.

- *When was the last time you testified in court?* While you may not need your financial planner to testify in court, it is an indicator of experience.
- *Are your credentials or licensing subject to review by government or regulatory agencies?* The answer should be yes.
- *Do you have any disciplinary events, suspensions, or violations on your record under this or any other name?* The answer should be no.
- *Are you currently licensed and in compliance with all appropriate governing regulatory agencies?* The answer should be yes.

Establish and Build Your Credit

If you are employed and/or already have credit cards in your name, the process of building your credit will be relatively straightforward. Use your credit cards regularly, pay off the balance on time each month, and your credit score will rise. However, if you're not employed and don't already have a credit history in your name, or if your credit is lousy, the process is not as simple. New federal regulations are making it more difficult than ever for women with little or no income to establish credit on their own, so prepare yourself for the possibility that securing credit or improving it could be somewhat time-consuming and is likely to require more than simply filling out an application or making a single phone call.

To have a FICO score, for example, you need at least one account that's been open six months or longer, and you need at least one creditor reporting your activity to the credit bureaus in the last six months. (A VantageScore, from FICO's biggest competitor, can be generated more quickly.)

Several tools can help you establish a credit history: secured credit cards, a credit-builder loan, a co-signed credit card or loan, or authorized user status on another person's credit card. Whichever you choose, make sure you use credit in a way that will eventually earn you a good credit score.

Five Ways to Establish Credit

Apply for a secured credit card

If you're building your credit score from scratch, you'll likely need to start with a secured credit card. A secured card is backed by a cash deposit you make upfront; the deposit amount is usually the same as your credit limit. You then use the card like any other credit card: Buy things, make a payment on a bill, and incur interest if you don't pay your balance in full. Your cash deposit is used as collateral if you fail to make payments. You'll receive your deposit back when you close the account.

Secured credit cards aren't meant to be used forever. The purpose of a secured card is to build your credit enough to qualify for an unsecured card — a card without a deposit and with better benefits. Choose a secured card with a low annual fee and make sure it reports to all three credit bureaus: Equifax, Experian, and TransUnion. NerdWallet (www.nerdwallet.com) regularly reviews and ranks secured credit card options.

Apply for a credit-builder loan

A credit-builder loan is exactly what it sounds like — its sole purpose is to help people build credit. Typically, the money you borrow is held by the lender in an account and not released to you until the loan is repaid. It's a forced savings program of sorts, and your payments are reported to credit bureaus. These loans are most often offered by credit unions or community banks.

Get a co-signer

It's also possible to get a loan or an unsecured credit card using a co-signer. But be sure that you and the co-signer understand that the co-signer is on the hook for the full amount owed if you don't pay.

Become an authorized user on someone else's credit card

A family member may be willing to add you as an authorized user on his or her card. As an authorized user, you'll enjoy access to a credit card and you'll build credit history, but you aren't legally obligated to pay for your charges.

Ask the primary cardholder to find out whether the card issuer reports authorized user activity to the credit bureaus. That activity generally is reported, but you'll want to make sure — otherwise your credit-building efforts may be wasted.

You should come to an agreement on how you'll use the card before you're added as an authorized user. If the primary cardholder expects you to pay your share, make sure you do so even though you aren't legally obligated.

Get credit for the rent you pay

Rent-reporting services such as RentTrack (www.renttrack.com) and Rental Kharma (www.rentalkharma.com) take a bill you are already paying and put it on your credit report, helping to build a positive history of on-time payments. Not every credit score takes these payments into account, but some do, and that may be enough to get a loan or credit card that firmly establishes your credit history for all lenders.

Build Your Credit Score with Good Habits

Building a good credit score takes time, probably at least six months of on-time payments. Practice these good credit habits to build your score and show that you're creditworthy:

- Make 100 percent of your payments on time, not only with credit accounts but also with other accounts, such as utility bills. Bills that go unpaid may be sold to a collection agency, which will seriously hurt your credit.
- Keep your credit card debt low. If possible, pay your balance in full each month, but if you do carry a balance

from month to month, don't let your debt balance exceed 30 percent of your credit limit.

- Avoid opening too many new accounts at once; new accounts lower your average account age, which makes up part of your credit score.

- Keep accounts open for as long as possible. Unless one of your unused cards has an annual fee, you should keep them all open and active for the sake of your length of payment history and credit utilization.

Check Your Credit Reports and Scores

As you take steps to build your credit, check your credit reports and score regularly. You're entitled to one free credit report every twelve months from each of the three bureaus. You can also get your reports at AnnualCreditReport.com.

Your credit reports don't contain credit scores, but you can get them in several ways. Here are some free options:

- Several credit card issuers — including Discover, Citi, and Barclaycard US — print your FICO score on your monthly statements and allow you to access it online. Discover goes one step further and offers a free FICO score to everyone, not just customers, at Credit Scorecard (www.creditscorecard.com).

- A few lenders — including Hyundai, Kia, Pentagon Federal, and Sallie Mae — also provide borrowers with ongoing access to their scores.

- Some websites offer free credit scores online, though they are typically VantageScores, rather than FICOs. But a good score on one scale is generally reflective of a good score on the other.

- Capital One offers a free VantageScore to anyone, cardholder or not (https://creditwise.capitalone.com).

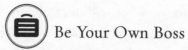 Be Your Own Boss

If you are serious about taking back your power, there is simply no better way to do it than to start your own business. Given the new economic reality of our time, more people than ever have found that the "job" they thought was waiting for them doesn't exist. If you have been out of the workforce for any significant period of time, you may realize that in order to have the flexibility you desire and the work you love after your divorce, you will need to create work that fits your needs.

Of course, if you are in the middle of a divorce, it probably isn't the right time to start a new business. However, it is a good time to think about it and plan for it. If you want to maximize your independence in your new life, brainstorm now about what it will take to launch your own business. That way, when you negotiate the divorce settlement, you can get what you need. It is never too early to lay the groundwork so that when the divorce decree is final, you are ready to go. See chapter 5, "Launch Your Own Business" (page 131), for more advice.

It doesn't matter what the motivation is to be your own boss. Many women have found out that it is very possible to earn what they need and enjoy themselves while doing it when they start their own business. Role models abound. As a mother of three, Melissa Kieling struggled finding a product to keep her kids' lunches cool and safe until lunchtime. So she patented the idea for a lunch bag with a freezable gel built into its lining — and that idea grew into PackIt Personal Cooler. Five years later, PackIt had grown into a $14-million business with products that spanned the lunch, wine, baby, picnic, and shopping categories and with distribution that included more than forty countries internationally.

Don't let inexperience stop you. Melissa's business résumé was basically limited to school bake sales. At first, not knowing which steps to take nearly paralyzed her with fear. She overcame this by reaching out to other business owners who could connect her to experts in manufacturing, production, and sales. Each key person she met shortened her learning curve and gave her confidence.

Nusha Pelicano is a single mother, an IRONMAN competitor, and a franchisee with Orange Leaf, the frozen-yogurt company. Pelicano opened her first Orange Leaf location in 2010. Today, she has five locations and another store on the way. As these women will attest, starting your own business is a surefire way to create freedom and independence in your new life. Here are the steps to get started.

Take a Stand for Yourself

Change can only occur when you make a conscious decision to make it happen. I was not naturally entrepreneurial. I spent my career working for a large corporate law firm, until it imploded during the recession. What seemed like a catastrophic event was one of the best things to happen to me, in that it forced me to go out on my own and start my own law firm. This in turn brought me independence and the good fortune to find my voice assisting other women who are navigating divorce. Decide now that you will not blame your ex, the economy, or anyone for your situation. Rather, use this opportunity to create something that will meet an unmet need. When you do this, abundance naturally follows.

Brainstorm

Give yourself permission to explore. Be willing to look at different facets of yourself (your personality, social style, age) and listen to your intuition. We tend to ignore intuition even though deep down we often know the truth. Ask yourself, "What gives me energy even when I'm tired?" How do you know what business is "right" for you? There are three common approaches to entrepreneurship:

- **Do what you know:** Look at work you have done for others in the past and think about how you could package those skills and offer them as your own services or products.

- **Do what others do:** Learn about other businesses that interest you. Identify businesses you like and what you like about them.
- **Solve a common problem:** Is there a gap in the market? Is there a service or product you would like to bring to market? (Note: This is the highest risk of the three approaches.) If you choose to do this, make sure that you become a student and gain knowledge first before you spend any money.

Start Planning Now

Most people don't plan, but planning will help you gain clarity, focus, and confidence. Start planning now, so that when the divorce decree is finalized, you are ready to go. As you write down your goals, strategies, and action steps, your business becomes real. For now, ask yourself the following questions:

- What am I building?
- Who will I serve?
- What is the promise I am making to my customers/clients and to myself?
- What are my objectives, strategies, and action steps to achieve my goals?

SELL BY CREATING VALUE

Even though we purchase products and services every day, people don't want to be "sold." Focus on serving others. The more people you serve, the more money you will make. When considering your customers or clients, ask yourself:

- What can I give them?
- How can I make them successful in their own pursuits?

This approach can help lead you to new ways to hone your product or service and deliver more value, which your customers will appreciate. When you are ready to turn your brainstorming into a business plan, turn to chapter 5, "Launch Your Own Business" (page 131).

 How and When to Tell Children You Are Divorcing

Many studies show that, as you might expect and may fear, children of divorced parents can develop into adults with lower self-esteem and more depression and anxiety compared to children who were raised by both parents. However, what studies also show, and what I emphasize with my clients, is that children are not typically damaged by divorce in and of itself. Rather, how parents handle the divorce, their conflicts, and their own emotions are what make the difference in how well children handle this difficult situation. Or as I like to say: Divorce is not damaging to children, conflict is.

No matter their age, a child's primary need is to feel safe and loved. Children struggle during divorce when they feel their security threatened. Of course, a divorce is upsetting for everyone, particularly for immediate family; to a degree, this can't be avoided. But similar to how you set the tone of a divorce by the way you notify your spouse, you set the tone for your children by the way that you inform them. I discuss this further in chapter 3, "Be the Grown-Up — Protect Your Children from Conflict" (page 76). Here I focus mostly on the first announcement.

First, what you say to your children and how you explain the divorce is up to you, and what you decide will no doubt depend on the age of your children, their maturity levels, and the particular circumstances of your divorce. However, I always advise that clients keep announcements and explanations as simple and succinct as possible. Avoid any information that children may not be equipped to handle, and avoid exhibiting conflict in front of them. Typically, the actual details of a separation are almost always emotionally charged, so shield your children from these.

I recommend that my clients tell their children that they are divorcing whenever they have made the definitive decision to do so, which is usually when they retain me. Don't put this off, and don't jump the gun. I've learned that a good way to present this decision is by saying, "We both love you very much, and we are going to be living apart." For young kids, this is often all that needs to be said, followed by showing them that you do indeed love them and that you are still a family. At first, avoid discussing the details of how this will work, especially if much still remains to be sorted out. Uncertainty causes anxiety, and one of your main goals during the divorce is to try to minimize anxiety for your kids. The most important thing they need to know is that they are loved (by both parents) and that they are safe.

You may feel tempted to say more than this. Particularly if you talk to your children without your husband present, you may want to explain yourself, seek sympathy, or blame your husband for the divorce. However, any bad things you have to say about your spouse can be emotionally turbulent for your children. For example, women often feel the need to talk to their children about their spouse's extramarital infidelity. Although it is tempting to bad-mouth your ex and his paramour to your kids, nothing good can come from this. This only puts children in the middle and forces them to choose allegiances. As I discuss in chapter 3, this can be incredibly damaging to children. Talk to your therapist or girlfriends about your spouse's extramarital activities, not your kids.

If, or when, your children ask you about the reasons for the divorce, answer them in a way that does not judge or criticize the other parent. Older children may be able to handle, and may appreciate being told, more details, but only when you can discuss the situation free of anger and blame. Remember, you don't have to explain everything to children right away. If you are still coming to terms with what happened, then you can't expect children to process that information in constructive, healthy ways, either. If children ask to know more, and you don't want to discuss it, perhaps reassure them that the reason you aren't discussing certain things is because they have nothing to do with them. As I discuss later, children will often blame themselves for a divorce, so make sure to emphasize that any conflict or negative emotions aren't because of them.

When a therapist colleague was asked by her young son why she was divorcing his father, she responded by saying, "Mommy and Daddy both love you, and we want you to be happy, and we want to be happy. We aren't happy in our marriage, and so we are going to change things for the better." Her son responded, "Mommy, I want you and Daddy to be happy." In other words, emphasize the positive.

As my father used to say when I was going through my separation and divorce, "The kids don't need to know how the sausage gets made." Remember this quote and keep any answers to questions from children short and sweet. Be honest, but spare them the details. This is one instance where less is more. Children also don't need to know all the details about your own uncertainty. However, you can't entirely shield children from the stress of a divorce, so pay attention to any signs of anxiety and stress, such as those listed in "Seek Help" below.

Tips for telling your children you are divorcing

- Tell children about the divorce together, if possible.
- Answer children's questions honestly, while avoiding unnecessary or upsetting details.
- Reassure children they are not to blame for the divorce.
- Tell children they are loved and will be taken care of.

 Check Alternative Housing Options in Your Area

One immediate question that arises when divorce proceedings start is where you both will live, both now and once the divorce is final. Who will get the house, or will you sell it and both move?

If you haven't decided, or before deciding, research your housing options by consulting MLS (Multiple Listing Service, www.mls.com), which is a free nationwide service providing real estate listings for sale or rent by member realtors (and other realty professionals) in your local community. The website features real estate news, common real estate questions, mortgage information, and a mortgage calculator. All kinds of properties are listed, and this is a good way to understand your housing options.

Find out what comparable homes are selling for and what you can expect to pay to rent or lease a home. This will assist you in determining whether to stay in your home, sell it now, or defer a sale (which you may prefer if you want to minimize the disruption for school-age children).

With your attorney, you can use this information, along with the information about your home's value (see "Learn the Fair Market Value of Your Home," page 25), to craft a strategy for keeping your home or using it as a bargaining chip in negotiations with your husband.

Seek Help

Divorce is challenging. You will undoubtedly be beset by a range of emotions, including denial, anger, depression, fear, resignation, ambivalence, and frustration. I have observed that if people tend to overeat, overshop, overdrink, or otherwise overindulge to numb painful feelings, these tendencies will be exacerbated. While numbing behaviors are common during a divorce, avoid excessive drug or alcohol use. These are never smart, and they may negatively impact your case. You can be sure that your husband and his attorney will highlight any negative habits in any proceedings in an effort to obtain an advantage. If so, you could be ordered to participate in random drug tests and lose custody or visitation of your children. Don't allow this to happen to you.

> **INSIDER TIP**
> *If you want to start therapy, do it now, so that it is included in your statement of monthly expenses. This is used to calculate the amount of support you will receive or have to pay. So not only is it wise to incorporate a mindfulness practice now, it is financially prudent!*

I advise all my clients to consult a therapist regularly during the divorce process for their mental and emotional health. As I've said, clients have a tendency to use their lawyer as their therapist, but this is a bad idea. For one thing, a lawyer charges much more per hour. So, if you haven't already done so, find a good therapist and see them regularly during your divorce. However, ensure the therapist supports your decision to end your marriage and is committed to helping you move through the process expeditiously — to survive divorce and thrive.

Find a Therapist for Yourself

As when looking for a divorce lawyer, I recommend that you interview three therapists before deciding, and seek licensed divorce therapists. Ask your girlfriends for referrals, especially those who have gone through divorce.

QUALIFICATIONS OF A LICENSED DIVORCE THERAPIST

Usually, individuals seeking to become a divorce therapist will start by earning a bachelor's degree in psychology, counseling, sociology, or social work with elective coursework focusing on marriage and/or family situations. Upon degree completion, most aspiring divorce therapists then go on to graduate school to earn a master's degree in marriage and family therapy (MFT), community counseling, or clinical mental health counseling. MFTs are held to strict licensure requirements, which include at least a master's level education in the field, or a related field, as well as a period of supervised clinical practice. In your interview, ask each therapist about their education and certifications.

THE IMPORTANT SKILLS THAT DIVORCE THERAPISTS NEED

When looking for a therapist, you want one who specializes in women facing divorce. You want someone who understands the stress you will feel as you navigate the legal process and work to reconstruct your life. That means, you want a therapist who either has been through divorce herself and successfully restructured her life or has helped many women going through divorce. For instance, I know one therapist who was having a difficult time finalizing her own divorce; the process went on for years, and it seemed to affect her therapy practice, since her clients also showed a tendency to wallow rather than to understand what happened and move on. You also need to feel that you can share your deepest feelings and darkest secrets with this person, so that they can effectively provide guidance. Divorce therapists also need solid organizational skills to maintain thorough case notes, keep detailed paperwork files, and manage insurance claims. Furthermore, divorce therapists often must work closely with spouses, children, family members, and other healthcare professionals, so strong collaboration skills are a must.

Find a Therapist for Your Children

Your children will also likely benefit from therapy during this time. Parents are often consumed with their own feelings and overlook the emotional state of the children, who may be confused by the divorce or feel guilt, loss, pain, or a sense of abandonment. It's common for children to feel they must "choose" a parent or to worry that they are the cause of the divorce. When divorcing parents fight, this impacts children, who often know when their parents are up-set, even when parents try their best to shield them. Therapy will provide a safe place for children to discuss their feelings about any issues that arise, whether as a result of divorce or not, and they may be able to process their emotions more easily and better adjust to the changes. For more on this, see "How to Handle Children Who Act Out" (page 110).

To find a therapist for your children, first discuss your children with your own therapist. Review any signs of stress identified in the lists below to determine if your children might benefit from therapy. Your therapist can probably recommend a therapist who specializes in working with children. Here again, you want some-one with credentials and who has experience working with children who are going through divorce.

How do you know when to seek help for your child?

If you are unsure whether your children need therapy, there are cer-tain red flags, or warning signs, that signal when it is time to seek the help of a professional. The following checklist provides some things to watch out for.

- Acting younger than their chronological age
- Showing fear of being apart from parent(s)
- Experiencing moodiness
- Acting out
- Being manipulative
- Experiencing sadness and depression
- Struggling with guilt
- Having sleep or eating problems
- Undergoing changes in personality
- Having academic and peer problems
- Displaying irrational fears and compulsive behavior

You might also consider having your children see a therapist if your divorce is particularly difficult. If any of the following occur, seek therapeutic help for your children as well as yourself:

- If you use the legal system to fight with each other.
- If one parent puts down or bad-mouths the other parent.
- If children are being used by either parent as message carriers or to spy on the other parent, causing children to feel caught in the middle.
- If you experience high levels of conflict with your spouse, where children repeatedly try to stop the fighting.
- If either parent relies on the children for a high level of emotional support and major responsibilities in the home.
- If either parent is experiencing depression or anxiety.

CHAPTER 3

Setting the Tone

"The tone is the message."

— Kevin T. McCarney

*T*he four hardest words to say to your husband are undoubtedly "I want a divorce." If you feel it's impossible to utter those words, you can have him served by a process server and avoid the confrontation. However, as Trish's story illustrates, surprising your spouse with divorce papers can set a negative tone for your entire divorce, which may not be in your best interest down the road.

Trish had been in marriage counseling with Daniel for four years and knew that the marriage needed to end. Despite her conviction, she just could not bring herself to utter those four words to Daniel's face, so she had him served at work with divorce papers. Daniel, a financial adviser, was embarrassed in front of his colleagues and staff. He was furious that Trish did not have the courage to tell him to his face that she was filing for divorce and that she chose instead to humiliate him at the office. Daniel retaliated by hiring the meanest pit bull of a lawyer that he could find, primarily out of revenge. The divorce was contentious and costly, partly because of how Trish set the tone.

In some limited instances, hiring a process server to serve your husband is wise, but there are a number of other ways to get the job done that are less likely to ramp up the contentiousness and keep things on a more even keel.

DIVORCE HACKS

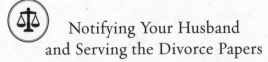 Notifying Your Husband
and Serving the Divorce Papers

INSIDER TIP
After telling your husband that you want to divorce, suggest that he sleep in another room, if he isn't already, or that he stay at a friend or family member's home until he can find his own place. I recommend that you stay in the family home with the children. Judges often enforce the status quo when making orders regarding custody, and if you leave the family home, they may rule that your husband gets to stay there with the kids.

As I say, if you want to minimize acrimony and keep your legal costs to a minimum, I recommend that you tell your husband in advance that you are filing for divorce, rather than surprise him with a process server. If you are in couples' therapy, that is often a "safe" place to have the discussion, especially if you're concerned about a volatile reaction. Regardless of where the discussion occurs, make certain your children are not present and will not hear. Keep the announcement short and to the point, and let your husband know that he will be receiving the divorce papers by mail from your attorney and that he'll need to retain counsel.

When Not to Tell Your Husband

You do not want to give your husband a heads-up that he is going to be served with divorce papers if you expect him to act in a selfish or vindictive way, like taking all the money out of the bank accounts or otherwise dissipating marital assets. In this case, have him served by a process server as soon as possible, and before indicating your intentions, because there are legal safeguards that come into effect once someone is served that preclude movement of money without permission or consent of the spouse.

The Process of Serving Divorce Papers

There are several options for serving the divorce papers, which you will want to discuss with your attorney. Regardless of how you decide to serve the papers, you cannot do it yourself. Serving papers must be done by someone other than you who is at least eighteen years old. The pros and cons of each method are outlined below.

OPTION 1: SENDING A NOTICE AND ACKNOWLEDGMENT OF RECEIPT

The least-aggravating way to serve divorce papers is by "notice and acknowledgment of receipt." Your attorney will send the summons, petition, and related documents by mail with a form that your husband will sign and return, acknowledging that he has been served. This is also the least-expensive form of service. This is a good option if there is no urgency to serve the papers, and you think your husband will cooperate by signing the document. If he doesn't cooperate or sign and return the form in a timely manner, then he is required to pay the cost to hire a process server.

OPTION 2: USING A PROCESS SERVER

If you are concerned that, upon learning you want a divorce, your husband may drain the bank accounts or dissipate marital assets, you need to have him served immediately. Once he is served with the summons and petition, automatic temporary restraining orders go into effect, and he can be held in contempt if he does anything that is outside the "ordinary course." In other words, the mortgage and other routine bills can (and should) be paid, but your husband cannot buy a house, take all the money out of the bank accounts, change the beneficiary on the life insurance, or cancel your or the children's health insurance. The main con of using a process server is that it can set a confrontational tone that affects the ensuing divorce proceedings.

I try to avoid using a process server whenever possible, but it is sometimes necessary. For example, for several weeks, Brigitte noticed that her husband was moving money from their joint accounts into his separate accounts and then transferring it to accounts overseas, where he owned property. He was also drinking a lot and had stopped going to work. She came to me wanting to file and worried about her husband's actions. I advised her to file immediately and to have him served by process without providing advance warning. As soon as she did, he admitted he was moving money in anticipation of a divorce, but he stopped right away and returned the funds to the joint account.

In another case, my client's husband cleaned out their joint checking account and simultaneously left the house with no warning. We filed and served him immediately and also filed a motion with the court to return the funds. Without having to appear in court, he returned the money to the joint checking account.

OPTION 3: SERVING PAPERS BY "PICKUP" DURING MEDIATION

If you have already decided jointly to mediate your divorce, then the mediator may prepare the petition and summons for "pickup." At separate times, the mediator will have each spouse come in to sign the divorce papers, thus effectuating service.

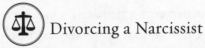 Divorcing a Narcissist

If you are divorcing a narcissist, buckle your seat belt. Narcissists are completely self-serving and selfish and utterly lacking in empathy. They will stop at nothing to "win." And if you have children, they are incapable of putting the children's best interest first. So, how do you get through a divorce unscathed if your spouse is narcissistic?

The only way to survive while divorcing a narcissist is to recognize who you are dealing with, roll up your sleeves, and adjust *your* behavior. The following advice will help orient you for the battle ahead.

The Characteristics of a Narcissist

How do you know if you are married to, and must now divorce, a narcissist? Lots of behaviors qualify as narcissism, and unless you are a psychiatrist, you aren't making a clinical diagnosis. Rather, if you recognize your husband in the list below, consider using the tactics that follow. Narcissism typically includes one or more of these attributes:

- A need for admiration
- A need to be right
- A need to be seen as the good person
- A need to criticize when others don't meet their needs
- Charisma and an ability to fool people
- A lack of remorse
- A lack of conscience
- A tremendous need to control others and the situation
- Situational values (they express the same values as those they want to impress, whether they believe in those values or not)
- A facade of caring and understanding used to manipulate
- Emotional unavailability
- Unwillingness to accept blame
- Tendency to hang on to resentment
- A grandiose sense of self
- Tendency to feel misunderstood

- A lack of interest in compromise
- Envy of the success of others

During a divorce, a narcissistic husband typically acts in a few specific ways: He completely dismisses any of your needs, or all the years of devotion and mutual companionship that you built together. Most people, even when they are angry and in conflict, remember the good from the past. They have a sense of balance and fairness. Even though they are getting a divorce, they recognize their valuable memories and life together. For the narcissist, it is all gone, like it never happened. Further, a narcissist may undermine you with your friends and your children, and steal your money, all while maintaining a facade of sincerity and goodwill with others. To deal effectively with a narcissist, anticipate these behaviors.

Tactics for Divorcing a Narcissist

A narcissistic husband will find it hard to accept that his influence in your life is over. Whoever filed for divorce, the narcissist will attempt to remain in control and keep influencing your life. If you have children, your husband will work overtime attempting to control how child support is spent, how visitation is handled, and every other aspect of the coparenting relationship. He will not put the children's needs first.

Depending on the situation, this behavior can amount to emotional, financial, and sometimes domestic abuse. Further, this abusive behavior will continue unless you stop it, so protect yourself. A narcissist will manipulate and feed off of any expression of sympathy, fear, weakness, or confusion, so avoid these. Protect yourself by showing no weakness, not buying into anything the narcissist says, understanding as much as you can about narcissistic behavior, and hiring an attorney who is willing to pull out all the stops when it comes to protecting your legal rights.

ADJUST TO, DON'T TRY TO CHANGE, A NARCISSIST'S BEHAVIOR

When we are in conflict with someone, it's natural to question ourselves — to ask to what degree our behavior is causing the problem and how we might act differently to change the other person's response. A narcissist is adept at manipulating this impulse and causing confusion. During a divorce, a narcissist will want you to be confused and questioning yourself. They will intentionally try to push your buttons, to make you angry, so that you do feel at fault, guilty, ashamed, and responsible.

Don't give in to this manipulation. Don't do or say things in order to change how your husband acts or responds to you. You cannot change the behaviors or attitudes of others. All you can control is the way you behave.

So be your best self. Be measured in your responses. Know that what a narcissistic husband does or says is not about you; it is about him. He is attempting to make himself feel better by projecting his own negative feelings onto you. This won't change no matter what you do.

BELIEVE IN YOURSELF AND IGNORE CRITICISM

The world of the narcissist is made up of fantasy; everything is an expression of their need to be someone they are not. Recognize this, and don't fall into the trap of *wishing* your husband was the kind of good person he pretends to be.

This is an inconvenient but important truth. The more you try to bring goodness out in them, or try to earn their good opinion, the more the narcissist will exploit that impulse.

The narcissist wants you to doubt your own value. So the best defense is to believe in yourself and your own self-worth and to ignore your husband when he criticizes, dismisses, or belittles you and your needs.

SET AND MAINTAIN CLEAR, FIRM BOUNDARIES
FOR COMMUNICATION

Narcissists believe their needs are more important than those of others. They believe they are more intelligent, and they find it unacceptable that anyone would disagree with them. For this reason, they lack an understanding of and respect for boundaries and the needs of others.

However, just because a narcissist doesn't respect boundaries doesn't mean you shouldn't set them. You should. The key is how you manage those boundaries. For instance, you can't expect a narcissist to respect your boundaries. He will keep crossing your boundaries. He does this with a few goals in mind: to get you to give them up, to make you mad and confrontational, and to manipulate you into trying to control his behavior by adjusting yours.

Don't make the mistake of doing any of those things. Set clear boundaries for communicating, and don't bend them. Don't become angry or confrontational, or aggressively assert your position, whenever those boundaries are crossed. And don't do anything to try to control what your husband does. This only plays into his game.

When setting boundaries with a narcissist, simply refuse to communicate unless it can be done in a manner free of conflict, manipulation, and disrespect. You may need to insist that all communication be via email. You might state that you will not respond to any communication that you feel dismisses or belittles you and your needs.

Expect the narcissist to push back against whatever boundaries you set. Expect it and don't try to change that. Boundaries are a threat to a narcissist. Just be firm, stand your ground, and refuse to be drawn back into the toxicity of the relationship.

SURROUND YOURSELF WITH AN UNDERSTANDING
SUPPORT SYSTEM

During divorce, we all turn to family and friends for support and advice. However, narcissists are skilled at charming others and hiding their behavior, and if this is true among your friends and family, they may not understand the extent of the abuse you are dealing with. When divorcing a narcissist, everyone you expect or hope to be on your side may not be.

So it is essential that you hire a divorce attorney who has an understanding of narcissistic personality disorder and how to deal with it during divorce. Also work with your therapist to help you set boundaries and stick with them. Your therapist can help you identify your role in the conflict and can help you understand what is and isn't "real." The people you turn to for help will play an important role in how well you navigate divorce from a narcissist.

 Establishing the Marital Standard of Living

The marital standard of living is the starting point for determining the amount and duration of spousal support. Your attorney and financial planner will work together with you to quantify your marital standard of living, which the court will rely upon in determining spousal support. The marital standard of living is not codified, and it's rather vague. It is typically defined as "the general station in life enjoyed by the parties during their marriage."

Trial courts ordinarily look to actual expenditures made during marriage to determine the marital standard of living. The court should also take into account the history of marital savings, which can be viewed as future expenditures. The marital standard of living is equal to income if the parties spend all their available income. The marital standard of living is also equal to income if the parties live beyond their means by financing their marital lifestyle. A more thorough analysis and presentation may be required in the event the parties did not spend all their available income during marriage.

The table below is an example of the type of presentation that should be prepared. This shows the types of financial information that your attorney and financial adviser will require in order to create an analysis of your standard of living and demonstrate the level of spousal support required.

Supported Spouse's Marital Standard of Living (MSOL) Analysis

EXPENSE	ANNUALLY	MONTHLY
Mortgage	$24,000	$2,000
Property taxes	$6,486	$541
Homeowner's insurance	$494	$41
Home maintenance	$600	$50
Home repairs	$6,000	$500
Utilities	$2,500	$208
Phone, cable, internet	$2,244	$187
Automobile expenses	$5,164	$430
Health insurance	$4,200	$350
Unreimbursed medical expenses	$936	$78
Food at home	$9,600	$800
Food eating out	$6,000	$500
Dry cleaning	$720	$60
Clothing	$1,800	$150
Personal	$2,892	$241
Fitness	$900	$75
Entertainment	$1,800	$150
Gifts	$900	$75
Vacations	$5,000	$417
Charitable contributions	$250	$21
Savings, investment, retirement	$13,000	$1,083
Federal and state income taxes	$13,680	$1,140
TOTAL EXPENSES	**$109,166**	**$9,096**
(Minus supported spouse's current earnings)	-$59,458	-$4,955
(Minus investment income)	-$7,236	-$603
SPOUSAL SUPPORT NECESSARY TO REPLICATE MSOL	**$42,472**	**$3,539**

Financial Information to Gather

As in the example above, to establish the marital standard of living, your legal team will need a detailed accounting of your annual and monthly expenses. Except for one-time costs, or costs billed annually (like property taxes and dues), all expenses should be calculated over the course of the previous year of the marriage up to the date of separation.

Here are the types of information to gather:

- Mortgage statement
- Property tax statement
- Homeowner's insurance statement
- Homeowner's association dues statement
- Home maintenance (include checks, credit card statements, and receipts)
- Home repairs (include checks, credit card statements, and receipts)
- Utilities statements
- Phone, cable, and internet statements
- Automobile expenses (include car loan payments, gas, and service records)
- Health insurance statement
- Unreimbursed medical expenses (include records)
- Food at home expenses
- Food eating out expenses
- Dry cleaning receipts
- Clothing expenses
- Personal expenses
- Fitness expenses (total account withdrawals for membership)
- Entertainment expenses
- Gifts
- Vacations
- Charitable contributions (average from past three years of income tax returns)

- Savings, investment, and retirement account contributions
- Miscellaneous (any other expenses that support your marital standard of living)

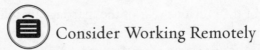 Consider Working Remotely

While this option isn't available for everyone, I recommend working remotely if possible, at least part of the time, while going through your divorce. Doing so will allow you to get your work done, to be more available to your children, to focus on the tasks your lawyer will give you and that you need to undertake to restructure your life, and to take some time for yourself.

I worked from home during my divorce, and for several years afterward, and I found this allowed me to focus on work while the kids were in school and then to be available to take them to their activities after school. I also had more time to get to yoga or the gym, since I wasn't wasting hours commuting back and forth from the office. Overall, this single change in how I approached work had the greatest positive impact on my quality of life while I was in the throes of my divorce.

You may be able to convince your current employer to allow you to work remotely at least part of the time. Ask your employer what they will allow. More and more companies are allowing employees to work remotely, since this can minimize overhead costs and improve quality of life for workers. Employers are realizing that it doesn't matter where an employee is, as long as he or she can communicate with the team and get work done. And if you are just starting your job search, look for companies that embrace remote work.

Since you may be reexamining where you want to live during

your divorce, going remote gives you more options. In theory, you can live almost anywhere, as long as the internet is fast enough.

Working Remotely in Your Current Job

Here are some things to consider when talking to your current employer about working remotely or when looking for a job that allows this.

TOUT YOUR ABILITY TO GET THINGS DONE AND TO BE A SELF-STARTER

A remote work environment encourages performance — not presence. Remote workers know their work style, their rhythms, how to self-start, how to stay on task, and how to stay inspired. They are excellent at communication.

FAMILIARIZE YOURSELF WITH VIRTUAL MEETING OPTIONS

Meetings, in some form, are important. Many times, you simply can't make effective decisions unless you hold a meeting. This is often a main reason employers discourage working remotely. If that's the case for you, suggest the employer try one of the free online services that help you do it, such as join.me or Skype. These allow communication and meetings without everyone needing to be in the same office. Project management applications such as Asana and Basecamp allow teams to stay up-to-date on projects, and chat functions such as Slack encourage live chatting. If you're interviewing for a remote position, familiarize yourself with these tools.

GO PAPERLESS

Most businesses have already "gone paperless" to a large degree. If you want to work remotely, you will definitely need to become comfortable sharing electronically through Google Docs or Dropbox.

Make sure your home internet service provider allows sufficient storage in the cloud.

Finding a New Remote Job

First, check out job boards like We Work Remotely (www.wework remotely.com) and Genesys (www.genesys.com), which allow employers to post jobs for people who are specifically interested in remote work. Both of these websites cater to start-ups and to companies that sell digital goods and services.

Indeed, the most remote-friendly businesses are those that have absolutely zero physical deliverables. The present and future of our knowledge worker industry is built upon the power of software, services, consulting, technology, and thought. If you want to work remotely, consider working with a service or product that is entirely digital. An example is Author Accelerator, a company that provides online coaching for aspiring authors. Jennie Nash is the owner of Author Accelerator, and her entire team of managers and book coaches works virtually. Team meetings are held using Uber-Conference, which is an online video chat room; tasks are tracked and assigned using Asana, a project management software; and daily communication happens on Slack, a real-time chat program.

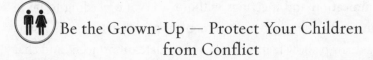 Be the Grown-Up — Protect Your Children from Conflict

When parents divorce, mothers typically set the tone of the divorce for children. Child-rearing typically falls heaviest on mothers, and this is particularly true during a divorce. It is an unavoidable fact — as mothers we enjoy that advantage and bear that burden. So how you handle your emotions is going to directly affect your children's well-being — now more than ever.

During a divorce, both parents often experience angry, resentful, and bitter feelings toward each other, and they may engage in vindictive behavior and even use the children as weapons in their battle. Sadly, the true victims of this type of behavior are the children.

Studies have shown that divorce *per se* is not the main cause when children experience problems in divorced families. The level of conflict is the main issue. For instance, families with married parents who are high-conflict have shown more child-adjustment problems than divorced families who are not high-conflict. Other studies have shown about half of the behavioral, achievement, and emotional problems seen in boys from divorced families could be identified as early as four years prior to the divorce; that is, parental conflicts were affecting children long before those conflicts led to divorce. So, to care for and protect children during a divorce, seek to minimize parental conflict. In fact, I found that once I got through my divorce, it was much easier to parent in a peaceful home than in an unhappy married home.

The level and type of conflict makes a difference. Parental conflict during divorce is more harmful for children when it is frequent; when it is heated and hostile, involving verbal insults and raised voices; when parents become physically aggressive; when parents withdraw from an argument or give each other the silent treatment; and when it's about the child. From an early age — research has shown as early as six months — children show distress when their parents fight. And anxious children are at higher risk of experiencing a variety of health problems, disturbed sleep, and difficulty in focusing and succeeding at school.

> **WISE WOMEN KNOW**
> *It's not divorce that harms kids, it's conflict. When we handle divorce well, our kids learn to handle divorce well.*

When children are distressed, they may externalize their feelings in the form of aggression, hostility, antisocial and noncompliant behavior, delinquency, and vandalism. They may internalize it in the form of depression, anxiety, and withdrawal. Over time, children who experience continued stress are more likely to have poor interpersonal skills, problem-solving abilities, and social competence. When these problems go unchecked, they can continue into adolescence and adulthood. For more advice on helping children who exhibit signs of stress, see "How to Handle Children Who Act Out" (page 110).

As you know, the stakes are high for your children. Thus, dealing in healthy ways with your anger and frustration with your spouse is important for the health and well-being of both yourself and your children.

I have seen many cases in which parents wage bitter custody battles against each other. In these battles, one parent attempts to obtain sole custody of the children while severely restricting the visiting rights of the other parent. When this happens, you might believe that one parent is trying to protect the children from an abusive spouse, one who is an alcoholic, addicted to drugs, or violent with the children. However, in too many cases, this isn't what's going on. Rather, the motivation of the vindictive parent is to exact revenge against the other parent for sins committed between the two of them and that have to do only with their relationship. For example, a betrayed wife may feel so upset that she is swept away by anger, rage, and the desire to punish the former spouse, and so she demands sole custody of their kids.

Another scenario is when one or both parents attempt to turn their children against the other parent. They will do all they can to devalue and demonize the other parent in the eyes of children. Parents put children in the middle of their conflict and encourage them to take sides, hoping to win children permanently to their side and against the other. I have witnessed the devastating effect this can have on children. For example, Michelle was so upset when Michael left her for a younger woman that she encouraged her teenage daughters to wage a Facebook battle against both their dad and his new girlfriend. As Michelle intended, Michael became estranged from his daughters, but both daughters suffered. Away at college for the first time, one daughter became deeply depressed and eventually dropped out of school. Children *never* benefit when they are drawn into marital conflict, regardless of their age.

To me, perhaps the worst-case situation is when, after divorce, the mother gains custody, the father moves away, and a curtain of silence falls between the children and the absent father. This occurs less often today, since courts now encourage shared custody, but it does happen, and with tragic consequences for the children.

A recent case is a sad example of how bad things can get. Carol was a devoted mother and stay-at-home mom to her three children, ages seven, eleven, and thirteen. When she learned Patrick had been repeatedly unfaithful, she filed for divorce. Within a month of filing, Patrick introduced the kids to his current girlfriend and insisted that the kids interact with her during his visitations. The two daughters, ages eleven and thirteen, rebelled and refused to spend time with their dad. The son, age seven, checked out and resorted to playing games on his phone whenever he was with his dad.

Carol was furious. It was obvious to everyone except Patrick that this arrangement was not in the children's best interest. However, the court ruled that Patrick have substantial visitation with the children, and it refused to get involved with how the time was spent.

Carol's anger and fury spilled over to the kids. She constantly bad-mouthed Patrick and the girlfriend, making it even harder for the kids to spend time with their dad. When they refused to go, Patrick resorted to calling the police to enforce the visitation order — a situation that ended up being deeply traumatizing for everyone.

Navigating Conflict and Your Feelings with Children

Since you can't avoid feeling conflict yourself when you are going through a divorce, how should you handle yourself around children? First, remember that children identify with each of their parents. If they are made to believe that one parent is evil, they may come to internalize this negative message about themselves. After all, they are the child of both parents, so if one is a bad person, then they must also be bad, at least in part.

Second, it is common for children to blame themselves for a divorce or otherwise believe that parental conflict is about themselves. They don't have the experience or context to understand what is happening between alienated parents, so they can personalize events that have nothing to do with them. They may do this even when parents assure their children that they are not to blame. A child might believe that one parent is leaving home because they do not love the child. If a parent leaves the home, a child may come to fear that they will have to leave home forever, too. Children may pretend that they do not care that one parent has left and throw themselves even more upon the parent who is present. These things can happen with kids of any age, but with young children especially.

Silence, distance, and a lack of contact — such as when one parent is successfully blocked from participation in the children's lives — can have the most significant consequences. When children have no information and are left to imagine what became of the missing parent, it is easy to imagine that they themselves are at fault.

Thus, it is really important that divorcing parents communicate two essential messages to their children: that they are loved by both Mom and Dad, and that the divorce is not caused by the children. As I recommend in chapter 2, keep these explanations as simple as possible. However, the message of your ongoing behavior can become even more important than what you say. Practice communicating confidence — in the other parent, that you and the children and your family will survive and thrive — and keep telling and showing your children they are safe with and loved by both parents.

Here are some other bad habits and negative actions to avoid around children during your divorce:

Do not blame, trash-talk, or complain about
your ex with your kids

When you are angry about a divorce, one of the hardest things is to avoid complaining about your spouse with your kids. However, even if your ex is a deadbeat dad, keep quiet about that in front of them. Watch out for the telltale possessive pronoun *your*, as in "*Your* father never does *X* or *Y*," or "*Your* father really messed up again," or "*Your* father is the reason I'm upset (or broke)," and so on. Anger, blame, bitterness, and resentment come through every time you utter a sentence like these.

Though you might not mean to, these complaints put your children in an emotional bind, and your children may become filled with resentment and guilt — that's their *parent* you're talking about! If your children agree with you, then it damages their relationship with their dad; if they don't agree, then it puts them in conflict with you. Just putting them in this position might jeopardize your relationship with your children down the line. After all, they ideally want to love both of their parents, and if they love and appreciate your ex, *you* could end up looking like the bad guy for bad-mouthing him.

If your ex is truly a deadbeat and deserves to be flogged for his behavior, let your children figure this out on their own and in their own time. They don't need to know, for instance, that the reason you can't take a vacation this year is because your ex isn't paying his child support and alimony. Acknowledge that finances are tight, and not entirely in your control, and then let them be children.

Further, and maybe most of all, complaints can put your children in the position of having to comfort you or be your therapist. Is that what you want? No. They're children! Manage your emotions on your own, and save the tissues and heartache for your adult friends and therapist, not your kids.

Action Steps for Building a Positive Relationship with Your Children During Divorce

- *Set aside time to do things together that both you and your kids enjoy — get a manicure together, go on a hike, go for a bike ride, attend a sporting event, or go to the movies together.*
- *Start a new activity together: tennis or golf lessons, yoga, photography, cooking classes.*
- *Plan a fun "staycation" or day trip that everyone enjoys.*
- *Spend time together in nature.*
- *Find a local restaurant that everyone likes and make that your go-to place for dinner when you're too busy or too tired to make dinner.*
- *Bake cookies together on the weekend and then enjoy them while watching a movie together.*
- *On the weekend or at the start of the week, when your children are with you, sit down to dinner together and discuss what is happening in everyone's lives during the upcoming week — find openings in your schedules to do something fun together during the week that you can all look forward to.*
- *Read books to your children in the evening; or if your children are too old for that, read the same book they are reading and discuss it together.*
- *Set aside quality time to be available to your children that gives them the opportunity to open up and talk to you.*

Do not quash all attempts by your ex to spend time with the kids

If you're angry at your ex — for cheating on you, leaving you, or anything under the sun — you have every right to be hurt and angry. Do not let your bad feelings keep your kids from having a relationship with the other parent. Don't stand in the way or undermine his visitation.

For instance, if Saturday is Dad's night, don't make excuses or pretend "something important suddenly came up," and so now your ex can't see your kids on his night. If that "something" is not an actual emergency — but only an excuse for not allowing your ex to spend time with the kids — be the grown-up and let your ex have his time.

DO NOT USE YOUR CHILDREN AS MESSENGERS BETWEEN YOU AND YOUR EX

No child should be a go-between. Regardless of your child's age, tell your ex whatever you need to tell him yourself. You can send a text or email to avoid confrontation.

DO NOT SABOTAGE YOUR EX TO MAKE YOURSELF LOOK LIKE THE BETTER PARENT

Parenting is not a competition. No one gets an award for making the most money and giving the most gifts. Doing things that could hurt your ex with the sole intention of looking like the better parent, or simply to enjoy watching your ex struggle, means *you* are acting like a deadbeat.

This isn't about what your ex deserves, but about how you behave. If your ex is toxic and awful — don't waste your precious energy attempting to make things worse for him, or showing him up so that your kids will crown you the "Best Parent." Think about the behavior that this is modeling: that it's okay to destroy others, to be sneaky, and to downplay and degrade another person's self-esteem. That's not how you want your kids to behave, so don't behave that way yourself.

DO NOT COMPARE YOUR CHILDREN
TO THEIR FATHER IN NEGATIVE WAYS

It's no secret you hate your ex. But when your children act like your ex, do not say, "You're just like your father!" Your kids know this isn't a loving compliment. In fact, they understand it's your way of saying, "You are being terrible just like my ex." Does that mean you now hate your children, too? Or are you just comparing them to a loser? Neither feels good, so don't do it.

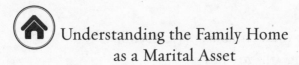

Understanding the Family Home as a Marital Asset

The decision about who gets the family home or whether to sell it is often one of the most difficult for women facing divorce. Attachment to the family home can be very emotional. If you have school-age children, the family home provides stability for them as they go through the transition of divorce.

I personally fought hard to stay in the family home because I wanted to provide stability for the kids and, frankly, for myself. After my ex and I separated, my kids and I lived there for over two years — in a large home I'd shared with my ex for ten years. Staying in the house was financially stressful, but I desperately fought to save it. I was finally forced to sell the house and had to downsize. I ended up renting a much smaller house in a new neighborhood, which I had been dreading for years.

I was astounded at what a positive experience it was to let go of the old and create a new living environment for me and the kids. The financial stress disappeared, and life opened up. The new house represented a fresh start. It had none of the painful memories from the end of our marriage. In our new smaller house, we were physically much closer together — my son built his Lego pirate ships in the kitchen while I made dinner. My daughter did her homework at the kitchen table while I cleaned up the dishes. All our bedrooms were together on the same floor next to one another. We grew much closer during this time as we created a new living environment tailored to our new family. When I look back at that time, I marvel at how vehemently I held on to the old house and how much freedom I experienced when I finally let it go.

Whether to keep the family home or sell it is a complex decision that includes emotional, financial, and tax consequences. It's wise to consider the overall situation and consult with experts who can provide you with objective advice about what the financial and tax consequences will be. This section, which discusses how courts handle the family home as a marital asset, and "Deciding What to Do about the Family Home" (page 107) will help you to evaluate your options and make a decision.

State law governs property ownership and asset division during a divorce. Your state will follow either community or equitable distribution property laws. For example, in a community-property state, you and your spouse will split marital assets in half. This could mean that you and your spouse are both entitled to 50 percent of the equity in the marital home. In an equitable distribution state, a judge will divide your property fairly — but that doesn't necessarily mean evenly or equally.

The date you acquired the house is an important piece of information in a divorce. Both in community and equitable distribution states, a judge can't award your separate property to your spouse. Property is usually designated as "separate" if it was a gift or inheritance or if it was acquired before the marriage. Generally, spouses keep their own separate property in a divorce.

> **INSIDER TIP**
> *You and your spouse can reach your own divorce agreement dividing up marital assets, including the family home. However, if you leave matters up to a judge, the parent with custody of minor children will probably get to stay in the marital home.*

A judge can award the marital home to one spouse as part of property distribution in your divorce. This assumes that the house qualifies as "marital" or "community property" and not one spouse's separate property.

A court will look at several factors to decide who gets the house. These factors may include, but aren't limited to, the following:

- Each spouse's financial circumstances
- Each spouse's contributions to the marital home
- Each spouse's age and physical and mental health
- Which parent has custody of the couple's minor children
- Source of funds for the marital home
- Each spouse's employability and job skills
- The value of the marital home

Dividing Equity in the Marital Home

In most divorces, the marital home is a couple's biggest asset. It's also the center of family life and often serves as an anchor for families with minor children. If a judge determines that the marital home is one spouse's separate property, the solution is simple: The spouse who owns it, gets it. It's a lot more complicated when the family home is a marital asset.

DISTRIBUTIVE SHARES WHEN THE HOME IS A MARITAL ASSET

A judge can award both spouses a share in the marital home. This means each spouse has rights to the value of the marital home. There are several ways to grant spouses their share of the marital home, such as the following:

- Requiring one spouse to pay for or "buy out" the other spouse's share.
- Awarding one spouse exclusive possession of the home for a limited period of time, and requiring the couple to sell the house by a certain date after that.

- Requiring the couple to sell the house immediately and divide the proceeds as directed by the court.
- Offsetting the value of the home by awarding additional marital assets to the other spouse.

DIVIDING A MARITAL RESIDENCE BY DEFERRED DISTRIBUTION

One way a court can divide a marital residence is by distributing the equity in your house on a future date, called a "deferred distribution." For example, a judge can award you the marital home to live in until your youngest child turns eighteen, at which point the house must be sold. Deferred distributions are also common in cases where the housing market is soft and divorcing couples want to keep their home until the market picks up. As part of a deferred distribution award, a court will usually require one or both spouses to cover maintenance fees, taxes, mortgage payments, and home owner's insurance.

 ## Essentials v. Nonessentials — Identify Priorities and Eliminate Nonessentials

During divorce, you are barraged by numerous tasks to get your life in order. I found that during my own divorce, I was forced to go against my perfectionist, OCD nature in order to move forward. There is great wisdom in learning that "good enough" is enough.

If you are committed to not just surviving but thriving, then learning to identify what is a true priority and eliminating nonessentials is critical. I remember during the darkest days of my divorce telling my mother that "this isn't working." What I meant was that my prior approach and philosophy of just working hard was no longer

> **WISE WOMEN KNOW**
> *"The sculptor produces the beautiful statue by chipping away such parts of the marble block as are not needed — it is a process of elimination."*
> — Elbert Hubbard

cutting it. I was in court with my ex about every six weeks, trying to get my business off the ground, and attempting to take care of three children and my mother, who was housebound after my father's unexpected and untimely death. Overwhelmed does not begin to describe what I was experiencing.

I was working as fast and as hard as humanly possible to keep everything going, but it wasn't working. I was falling apart — physically and emotionally. Through my mindfulness practice, I recognized this, and I came to understand that I had to completely restructure my approach to day-to-day tasks. I was forced to pare down my existence to what really mattered. Here is what I learned.

GET AN EARLY START

Let's face it, while going through divorce, you've got so much on your mind that you are probably not sleeping well. Combine that with likely hormonal fluctuations, and chances are you are waking up very early and then lying in bed in a cold sweat. Use this time! There is so much that can be accomplished in the early dawn hours while your children (and most other humans) are sleeping. If you are diligent, you can accomplish half a day's work before the rest of the world has rolled out of bed.

MAKE A LIST OF THE THINGS THAT MUST GET DONE EACH DAY

After your morning mindfulness practice, write down all the things that you must do that day. In no particular order, just write them all down.

PARE THE LIST DOWN TO FOUR TO SIX ITEMS

This is challenging, but it works. Force yourself to eliminate all but four (best) to six (max) items on your to-do list.

START WITH THE HARDEST TASK

This is a game changer. Start with the brain twister or the least-desirable task, and get it done while your energy is high. When you check it off your list, it will incentivize you to keep plugging away.

ELIMINATE WHAT'S NONESSENTIAL

If you want to accomplish what's essential, the four to six items you chose, then you must eliminate the rest, all the other items you left off the list. This is a hard one to wrap your brain around because most of us spend a great deal of time on things that don't matter. But letting go of what doesn't serve you is critical to your future happiness and success. When I took a hard look at this during my divorce, I found that I was spending an inordinate amount of time and money on things that really didn't matter — such as getting my eyebrows waxed and shopping for things we didn't really need. I restructured my life so that I could focus on becoming financially independent and on my children, and I cut out everything else. Consciously changing habits to eliminate the trivial and nonessential literally saved me from myself.

> INSIDER TIP
>
> *A very wise and successful man once told me, "Do anything that matters before noon." I took this advice to heart and shifted my morning workout to 4 PM, after my work was done. This single adjustment resulted in doubling my productivity and profits.*

ASK YOURSELF IN EACH MOMENT: IS WHAT I'M DOING CONTRIBUTING TO MY FREEDOM, INDEPENDENCE, AND HAPPINESS?

If the answer to that question is no, then stop doing it. You will be astonished at how many of the things we routinely do are nonessential and can be eliminated.

CHAPTER 4

Digging In

"Some people believe holding on and hanging in there are signs of great strength. However, there are times when it takes much more strength to know when to let go and then do it."

— Ann Landers

O nce you've announced your decision to divorce and the papers have been filed, it's time to roll up your sleeves and dig in. You need to gather information, prepare your financial disclosures, and make some tough decisions — all while managing your wide-ranging emotions and those of your kids. This can be a challenging time in the divorce process. You are going through the grieving process just as you need to drill down on a variety of tasks.

This is the stage in the divorce where some women freeze. They get stuck in denial, and it impedes their ability to do what they need to do to move forward. The antidote is to set clear boundaries and enlist your support system so that you can do what needs to be done while taking care of your emotional needs.

Carol arrived in my office with tears streaming down her face. She had brought a friend along for moral support. I'd asked her to complete her financial disclosures, which requires gathering information and preparing forms showing all your income, expenses, assets, and debts, but instead of using the time to complete this task, she spent the hour crying about the end of her marriage. I asked Carol whether she had a therapist — she did. But Carol was having difficulty focusing on the task at hand. I asked whether her friend could help her put together her financial disclosures. She was eager to help, and with that redirection, Carol was able to focus and take the necessary steps to move forward.

Follow the steps in this chapter to help you focus on what matters, allow yourself to process your emotions, and let go of the rest.

DIVORCE HACKS

 Preparing Your Financial Disclosures

Preparing and exchanging preliminary financial disclosures is a required step in the divorce process. Without the completion of this step, a judge will not grant a divorce. This documentation provides the parties, lawyers, and judge with a snapshot of the parties' income, expenditures, assets, and debts. It is used to determine the amount of spousal support, of child support, and the division of assets and debts. Negligent and willful omissions of assets and debts when preparing the preliminary financial disclosures can lead to devastating results. The importance of full transparency and disclosure cannot be overstated.

I've often been asked about whether it is important to disclose all items of income on the income and expense declaration. The short answer is yes! You must disclose everything. If you don't and it is discovered later, the consequences are severe. A now-infamous California lottery case is demonstrative. Denise Rossi won $1.3 million in the California lottery; did not tell her husband of twenty-five years, Thomas; and filed for divorce eleven days later. She did not disclose her winnings on her income and expense declaration, which specifically requires disclosure of all income earned in the past twelve months, including one-time awards, such as lottery winnings. She told no one in her divorce case.

More than two years after the divorce, a misdirected piece of mail landed in Thomas Rossi's mailbox. It was a solicitation addressed to his ex-wife from a company that pays lump sums for lottery winnings and big legal awards. Thomas scratched his head for a while, but eventually he confirmed that his ex-wife had won over a million dollars from the lottery. He learned that Denise's deception went so far as to have the lottery checks sent to her mother's address in Northern California. A Los Angeles family court judge ruled that she had violated state asset disclosure laws and awarded her *entire* lottery winnings to her ex-husband.

If Denise had disclosed the lottery winnings on her financial disclosures, Thomas would have had a community-property interest in the winnings and her attorney may have been able to negotiate something less than 50 percent. But because Denise concealed her winnings, she lost every penny.

In most states, you have sixty days after you file for divorce, or respond to the petition, to serve your financial disclosures, which includes an income and expense declaration and a schedule of assets and debts.

The income and expense declaration provides a monthly snapshot of your income from wages, investments, and other sources, and it also provides a schedule of your monthly expenses. The preparation of the monthly expense schedule is very important because it shows what your monthly need is for your household (for you and your children), and it is used to determine how much spousal support will be awarded. Whoever is the higher-earning spouse is the one who pays support, and these forms determine their ability to pay.

When you prepare your financial disclosures, be very careful and accurate. You can hurt yourself if you are sloppy and put down inaccurate numbers or withhold information. You should review your bank records and other financial documents closely. Don't estimate; use your actual bills, receipts, and credit card statements. For a list of the typical items to include, see "Establishing the Marital Standard of Living" (page 71) in chapter 3. Take a twelve-month look at your actual expenses so that you can account for seasonal variations. Seasonal variations affect utilities, fuel, and many other types of expenses that a one- or two-month snapshot will not take into account realistically. And don't forget to include one-time yearly expenses such as summer camp for the kids.

Your husband's attorney is going to scrutinize your financial disclosure statement using your bank records and the other documents that you are required to disclose. The court will do the same. You should start your preparation of a financial disclosure statement by carefully reviewing your financial records. This will ensure that your financial statement is as accurate as possible. This can have a very significant impact on your case.

INSIDER TIP
After filing for divorce, keep a record of any expenses for the children you have paid with your separate funds (such as your income received after separation or money from an inheritance). These expenditures are reimbursable — but you must be able to account for them at the end of your divorce.

While it may, at first glance, appear easy to identify the entire marital estate, the problem is this: Many women don't have an adequate understanding of their financial lives, tax law, or divorce law, and this causes some serious consequences. For example, a woman who came in for a consult after representing herself had listed the 401K in her husband's name as his separate property and the property that she inherited from her grandmother as community property. She had made these decisions, she told me, because she believed the 401K was not hers, since she had not earned it and it was in her husband's name, and since the inherited property was acquired during the marriage, she believed it was community property. She was prepared to settle with her husband as follows: He would keep "his" 401K, and they would split the value of the inherited property. She believed she had struck a very good deal. To the contrary, the husband had zero entitlement to her inherited property, and she had a 50 percent entitlement to all deposits made to the 401K during the period of marriage. Needless to say, she was happy with this new reality. I share this example because these kinds of mistakes are typical; I see them in my practice all the time. Many women don't understand the fundamental principles of divorce law and list their assets in a way that affords a windfall to the husband.

ACTION STEPS TO PREPARE FINANCIAL DISCLOSURES

- Calendar a deadline in four weeks to have a draft prepared to submit to your attorney for review. Don't wait till the sixty-day time period has nearly run out to begin preparing the financial disclosures. It takes longer to put them together than you think.
- For your income and expense declaration, use many of the same categories and figures that you use in your marital standard of living analysis (see "Establishing the Marital Standard of Living," page 71). Update these figures to reflect your current expenses for your household, which includes you and anyone who is living with you.

> **INSIDER TIP**
> *Fill out the forms in pencil. You will find that you forgot to include items and need to edit.*

- Take your time to make certain that you include all of your anticipated expenses. This is your "need," which attorneys and courts use to determine the level of support you will receive. If you leave something out, it is unlikely your ex-spouse will make up the difference once the divorce decree is final.
- Review utility payments and other fluctuating payments over the past twelve months and come up with an average for your expense statement.

- Include things like children's piano and tennis lessons, summer camps, fees for college entrance exams, and all extracurricular activities for the kids over the past twelve months (and divide these one-time expenses by twelve to come up with an average monthly expenditure).
- If you have children who will be heading off to college within the calendar year, include tuition, as well as all anticipated expenses for travel and to get them set up.
- List all assets regardless of the characterization. Even if you think that something may be separate property, list everything and review with your attorney.

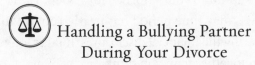 Handling a Bullying Partner
During Your Divorce

During their marriage, Victoria's husband, Paul, was charismatic and charming. But when the divorce got under way, Paul became a monster. He hired the meanest bulldog of a lawyer and threatened Victoria that he would take full custody of the kids. The more Victoria tried to reason with Paul, the worse it got. Then the cyberbullying began. Every time Victoria opened an email, Paul accused her of being a "terrible mother," an "idiot," and threatened to drive her into bankruptcy if she didn't cave to his demands. Victoria was in the midst of starting an online business. She was terrified that Paul would take his cyberbullying to the next level and trash her online. She couldn't sleep without antianxiety medication and she couldn't eat. Fortunately for Victoria, she wasn't defenseless. She took back her power and didn't give in. If your ex is bullying you, know what constitutes bullying and what does and doesn't work to counter it.

What Bullying Looks Like In a Divorce

Bullies habitually operate by playing on the fears of their victims, and unfortunately, there are few people who know more about you and your fears than an ex-partner. During a divorce, these are the typical ways an ex may try to bully you:

- Lying about past incidents in a way that makes you look bad.
- Making threats about taking full custody of the children and/or preventing you from seeing them.
- Attempting to isolate you from friends and family members.
- Hiring a lawyer for the purpose of intimidation.
- Harassing you with offending emails or by posting defamatory content online.

What Doesn't Work to Stop Bullying

You might think that reasoning with your ex to bring him to his senses will work. Wrong! Like a narcissist, a bully is unconcerned with anyone else's well-being. All that matters is regaining control of what feels like an out-of-control situation — by bullying you. While it may seem counterintuitive, the following things do not work to stop bullying; they only encourage a bully to continue.

- Pleas of fairness or reason — a bully will twist your responses and use them against you.
- Attempts to set the record straight — the facts do not matter to a bully.
- Signs of weakness or vulnerability — bullies prey on the weak.

How to Protect Yourself from a Bully

To deal with a bully, also review my advice for dealing with a narcissist (see "Divorcing a Narcissist," page 66). In essence, you can't control someone else's behavior, but you can set boundaries and take care of yourself.

SET CLEAR BOUNDARIES

Bullies don't respect the personal boundaries of others. And no one knows your boundaries, or lack thereof, better than your spouse. Another thing that's common to bullies is that they're almost always cowards; they bully people they perceive as weaker, often because they themselves feel insecure.

Setting boundaries is important. First, it's a way to stand up for yourself and make clear that you won't tolerate bullying behavior. Boundaries also create accountability. If you set clear boundaries, and these are later ignored, it's then impossible for your spouse to claim that their bad behavior was unintentional.

When you're being bullied, it's very common to feel as though you can't stand up for yourself. You may feel you have no way of holding your ex accountable for their actions. Combat this by keeping a record of each incident of bullying: the date and time on which it occurred, the medium through which it occurred (such as phone, email, in person), and the details of what happened. Give this information to your attorney so that they can determine whether to take legal action to stop the abuse.

For example, if your ex persists in coming to your house unannounced and uninvited, set boundaries by telling him in person and in writing that he's no longer welcome unless you specifically invite him. Or you can have your attorney send a letter to your spouse's attorney outlining the unwelcome and unannounced visits and clearly stating that they must stop. It's important to create a written record. Then, if you must go to court to obtain an order to stop the abuse, you have evidence to support your request.

TREAT HOSTILE EMAILS AND SOCIAL MEDIA POSTS AS CYBERBULLYING

Cyberbullying is harassment that takes place using any form of electronic technology. It is usually committed by email or on social media and is a form of harassment linked to stalking. The New York

State Division of Criminal Justice Services includes "hostile, vulgar, and insulting" emails in its definition of cyberbullying. It also includes impersonation and posting derogatory, embarrassing, and false information about a victim online.

If your ex is engaging in any form of cyberbullying, take the following steps:

- Clearly communicate that you want the contact to end and then *stop responding.*
- Print out a record of all communication.
- Block his account.
- Use privacy settings on social media.
- Unfriend him.
- Report him to the social media site.
- Make a report to the internet service provider (ISP), or the website moderator, and keep the record of your report.
- File a police report if you feel threatened.
- Provide the written record of bullying to your attorney.

Stay safe and consider a restraining order

A bullying partner isn't always an abusive one, and he isn't always a dangerous one. But if there's a risk that your ex might become violent in any way, take whatever steps you need to ensure your safety. The danger is highest for women who leave already abusive or violent partners. No matter what the situation, first and foremost, make sure you and your children are safe. If your safety is at risk, talk to your attorney about whether to file a restraining order.

Take care of your health

Being a victim of bullying can have long-term consequences for both physical and mental health. Mental health consequences can include depression and anxiety, insomnia, panic attacks, fearfulness, loss of self-esteem and confidence, and agoraphobia. In terms of physical health, common problems include headaches and muscle tension, digestive problems, fatigue, and increased frequency of illness.

Many victims of domestic abuse or bullying come to neglect their health, may eat less, become less physically active, and stop engaging in social activities. Be mindful if you find yourself doing the same things, no matter what your situation. As you move through a divorce, it's important to simply take care of your own health by eating nutritious food, exercising, and returning to activities that you once enjoyed. Double-down on your meditation practice. Make regular and frequent appointments with your therapist to work on managing your stress and setting clear boundaries.

Don't let yourself be rushed to finalize the divorce

A common bullying tactic is for one spouse to rush the divorce proceedings in an effort to force their ex to make an agreement that's unfavorable to them. They won't say this is the reason, of course. They might claim that they need the divorce to be completed quickly because they want to invest their share of the assets, because of tax consequences, or because they want to end the process as soon as possible for the sake of the children.

If you find yourself being rushed faster than you're comfortable with, remember that it's okay to slow down and take your time. You may want the divorce to be over quickly, too, but even so, it's important to make sure that assets are divided fairly — not just for your children, but for your own sake. Take the time you need.

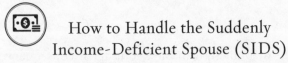

How to Handle the Suddenly Income-Deficient Spouse (SIDS)

As I've described, when husbands realize that divorce is a possibility, they tend to become self-protective of their finances. A moment comes, usually during marital counseling, and sometimes long before divorce is filed, when a husband's focus will shift from the fate of the marriage to his individual future, and he will start manipulating his finances with that in mind. Of course, today, husbands and wives often both work and earn incomes, but that doesn't mean a wife isn't vulnerable to financial maneuvering by a husband seeking to minimize his losses in a divorce. Husbands are still most commonly the higher-earning spouse, and many women are not always as knowledgeable about family finances as, frankly, they ought to be.

If a husband owns a business, this presents several opportunities for financial maneuvering. For example, once the divorce gets under way, husbands often claim that the business actually has little or no income or value. Despite the lifestyle the business has supported to now, suddenly it's in trouble, and this conveniently prevents a husband from paying his fair share of spousal or child support.

This happens so often that divorce professionals have a name for it: the Suddenly Income-Deficient Spouse, or SIDS. Here are some telltale signs of SIDS:

THE BUSINESS IS IN TROUBLE AFTER THE DIVORCE IS FILED

The husband's business has supported a very nice lifestyle for the family for quite some time. However, once divorce proceedings start, the husband claims he's drastically lost income — at the same time that he's bought a new Porsche, supported a new girlfriend in high style, and traveled all over the world (on "business"). Where's the money coming from?

THE BUSINESS PAYS THE HUSBAND'S PERSONAL EXPENSES

The husband's business pays his personal expenses, and he doesn't need to take a paycheck — so he claims he has very little income. He claims all his expenses (car, travel, entertainment, and so on) as "business expenses," which reduces his net income to virtually zero. This causes the business to appear to take a hit in value.

HIS LOSS OF INCOME BEGAN JUST AS
YOUR MARITAL TROUBLES WERE INTENSIFYING

Sometimes, husbands plan for divorce far longer than their spouse's imagine. In many situations, he may have been having an affair for over a year — sometimes longer — and been teeing up this financial charade the whole time. Then, right on cue, the business appears to take a hit just as the divorce is filed, but this is not accidental. Think back: Was there a turning point in your marriage that could have set him down that path? Did you split and get back together, before ultimately deciding to divorce? And did the business lose value right about the time you first separated?

HE STALLS OR STONEWALLS WHEN ASKED TO
TURN OVER FINANCIAL DOCUMENTS

If your husband is suddenly income-deficient, then it's likely he will be reluctant to turn over third-party data, such as bank and credit card statements, loan documentation, and copies of checks, all of which are difficult to manipulate. He'll want to buy time, while also driving up your legal bills by forcing your attorney to make repeated requests and demands for documentation you are legally entitled to. The sooner you're out of money to pay your divorce team, the sooner you'll settle for less than you deserve, just to get it over.

It can be difficult to prove that someone is underreporting income and/or misrepresenting the value of a business, particularly when the husband has control of all the financial information. To support your case, and create a credibility issue for your husband, you will need to prove that the financial picture of a losing enterprise is inconsistent with the evidence — the financial documentation.

You will probably need to retain a forensic accountant, who will work with your attorney to establish the inconsistencies in your husband's position. A forensic accountant is specifically expert in detecting inconsistencies, finding evidence of wrongdoing, and getting at the truth of a financial situation (see "How a Forensic Accountant Can Help," page 176).

Some crafty business owners start bad-mouthing their business's profitability a year or more in advance of the divorce. When they know divorce is on the horizon, business owners draw less income because they control their own compensation, and they simultaneously clamp down on personal spending to appear broke. Some even sell their luxury cars and buy compact cars. Others move out of the house and into a friend's guesthouse.

The way to uncover these types of scams is to have your attorney demand through formal written discovery that your spouse provide the business's financials and loan applications. Formal written discovery can include formally asking for documents ("request for production"), written questions ("interrogatories"), deposition (interrogating your husband under oath), and subpoenaing his business records from third parties (such as banks or employers). Your spouse must respond under oath and provide what is requested. The forensic accountant will review the personal and business tax returns and compare them to the business's financials to uncover inconsistencies.

In my experience, when I have taken this step for clients and deposed a Suddenly Income-Deficient Spouse, he will often cave and offer an acceptable settlement proposal without having to go to court. If he has lied on his tax returns by overstating his expenses, he will be more likely to comply. Requesting formal written discovery can therefore be an effective strategy for a wife seeking support and an acceptable settlement.

ACTION STEPS TO COUNTER A SUDDENLY INCOME-DEFICIENT SPOUSE

- As soon as you think your marriage is in trouble, gather personal and business tax returns for the past three years and, if possible, documentation of the business's financials.

- If you do not have access to this information, discuss with your attorney the need to take discovery to obtain it.

- Ask your attorney whether it is advisable to retain a forensic accountant to assist with the preparation and review of information obtained through discovery.

- Factor into your divorce budget the cost of discovery and bringing a forensic accountant on the team.

- If your husband is earning less than before or is suddenly unemployed, consider conducting a vocational evaluation (see below).

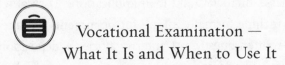

Vocational Examination — What It Is and When to Use It

In a divorce proceeding, information and evaluations from a vocational expert can be required by or presented to the court for consideration in determining spousal and child support payments. Vocational experts evaluate a person's abilities, interests, education, experience, and other qualifications against the backdrop of the current employment market. They assess the likelihood that a person can get a job, and what he or she can expect to earn, both immediately and in the long term.

If you're in the process of divorcing, or even if you're just thinking you may be headed down that path, here are three key reasons why you may need a vocational expert in your corner: to get a fair assessment of your husband's earning potential, to get a fair assessment of your own earning potential, and to provide the court with a second opinion should your husband ask for a vocational assessment.

To obtain an objective, professional assessment of your spouse's earning potential

Very often, a spouse with historically high earnings will nonetheless want his alimony and/or child support obligations to be determined based on a much lower income. Once in divorce proceedings, your husband may claim his earnings have plummeted due to current economic conditions. He may even quit his job or take a lower-paying position during the divorce, only so his alimony and child support payments will be less. These are underhanded tactics, to be sure — and they're particularly difficult to understand when child support is involved — but be aware: Husbands often use dirty tricks like these, and more often than most women realize.

Fortunately, a vocational expert can cut through devious strategies and false assertions. They'll objectively answer these critical questions: What can your husband reasonably be expected to earn? If his income has legitimately decreased, is it likely to rebound? How soon?

To get a realistic idea of your own employability and earning potential

A husband may insist his wife is fully capable of earning a six-figure income, even if she has been entirely out of the workforce for many years. This is an especially likely claim if she has advanced degrees or special training. In your situation, if you gave up paid work to care for your children, or if you are simply not working, you'll want to know what your employment prospects are and what you can expect to earn if you reenter the workforce. A vocational expert can tell you how your education and work history position will fare in today's job market, and whether you'll need additional training to update your skills. You might welcome this kind of career advice simply because it's helpful for personal and professional growth. In a divorce, having this knowledge under your belt is also a valuable defensive tactic. Vocational expertise can help ensure your settlement is calculated based on fair assumptions.

I've seen time and time again how some estranged husbands try to gain a financial advantage by demanding a vocational examination. If the evaluator finds that you could be earning a certain amount of money, and you are not, then the court will include that in its calculation of support, and it will reduce what your husband owes. However, a vocational evaluation can set the record straight. If you have been out of the workforce, the evaluator will provide valuable information about how long it will take you to obtain employment and what training and education you may need in order to get a job. This is useful information in coming up with a reasonable plan to assist you.

> INSIDER TIP
>
> *If you agree to submit to a vocational evaluation, have your attorney demand that your husband pay for it. It can be expensive (from $3,500 to $7,000, and more), and often he will agree to shoulder the cost if he is trying to force you back to work.*

What's more, you will likely find that the results of interest and aptitude tests from the vocational evaluation process can be valuable down the road. When the turmoil of the divorce is behind you, and you're setting new personal and professional goals as a single woman, you may choose to revisit a vocational consultant for guidance in making a career change or even launching your own business.

To provide another opinion if your spouse is retaining a vocational expert

In some states, a vocational evaluation is mandatory if one spouse is unemployed. In theory, this should be fair and impartial.

However, this doesn't always turn out the way you want. For example, if you are qualified to work in a field where jobs are available paying $50,000 a year, but you choose to work at a bookshop and earn $20,000, it is possible your husband's obligation to pay spousal support would be based on the $50,000 you "could" be earning.

In contentious divorce cases, both sides may bring in a vocational expert to be sure that the conclusions reached truly are reasonable, fair, and consistent. If you are required to cooperate with
a vocational evaluation requested by your spouse, it may be in your
best interest to have your own expert conduct one as well to provide
another opinion to the court.

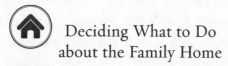

Deciding What to Do about the Family Home

In chapter 3, I discuss how courts treat the family home as a marital asset (page 84). Here, I drill down on the decision of whether
to stay or sell your family home. Often, women let their emotions
guide (or cloud) this decision, but I encourage you to evaluate the
financial repercussions of each scenario and to make the smartest
"business decision" given your situation. Here are the major issues
to consider.

Stability for the Kids: Deciding to Stay in the Family Home

Women in particular tend to be adamant about keeping the family home, which is often an effort to provide stability for the kids.
Stability is important for children during a divorce, but make sure
that the price isn't keeping an expensive home you can't afford.
Kids are also flexible, and if children remain in the same neighborhood and schools, so their friendships aren't disrupted, moving to
a new, smaller, and cheaper house or apartment might not affect
them as much as you think. If you feel strongly about keeping your
family home, take a close look at how you'll finance it and pay the
bills and the level of income you'll need. Another important way
to create emotional stability after a divorce is by living within your
means.

Finally, don't make the decision on your own or in a vacuum.
Get advice from your team: your attorney, financial adviser, and tax
adviser.

Can you afford the house on your own when the divorce is over?

Deliberating over what you can really afford can be painful. No matter how much you may want to stay in the home, your financial situation will likely become much tighter following divorce.

First, gather and review what is owed on the house and how much support you will need to make the payments. If refinancing the mortgage might lower your monthly payments, find out if you'll be able to qualify on your own income to refinance into your own name.

Then, draft a sample monthly budget and compare it to your likely postdivorce income (including any support). How hard will it be to make ends meet? Consider other future costs, like rising real estate taxes, home repairs, maintenance, and landscaping. These can chip away at your new single-person budget, making it harder to save for other things as you start your new life.

Bargain other marital assets to make owning your home affordable

Determine whether there are assets you can trade during settlement negotiations in exchange for the house or to lessen your monthly payments. Depending on what those things are, is it worth giving them up in order to keep your family home?

Keep the tax consequences of your future home sale in mind

If you keep the house now and sell it on your own later, you could end up with a hefty capital gains tax bill, depending on how much your home sells for at that later time. Figure these future taxes into your settlement agreement. Get advice from a tax accountant or Certified Divorce Financial Analyst, who can weigh the various short- and long-term tax consequences of different scenarios and help you decide which assets and liabilities to trade or bargain with during divorce.

CONSIDER PLANNING FOR A DEFERRED SALE OF THE FAMILY HOME

As I've mentioned, divorced parents often decide to defer the sale of the family home until children turn eighteen. In some situations, this can be the best of both worlds. The children get to remain in the family home till they're ready to leave, and the terms of the home's future sale are negotiated and accounted for in the divorce settlement. If you want to defer the sale of the house, have your lawyer negotiate so that your husband shares payment for ongoing improvements and maintenance, since he'll benefit when the house is ultimately sold.

A Fresh Start: Deciding to Sell the Family Home

If you sell your home, there won't be any worry about whether or not either person can qualify on their own income to refinance it into their own name. You can use your share of the profit from the home sale to prioritize your new financial goals. You won't find yourself late at night in the kitchen, remembering that terrible fight you had right before it became clear you needed to divorce. Being open to new possibilities may lead you to downsize, buy a fixer-upper, try an entirely different floor plan, or move into a new community where you and only you have the keys to unlock your front door. Best of all, you will have a fresh start.

There are really two main questions to answer if you decide to sell: What profit can you expect from the home sale, and what will it cost to move and live somewhere else?

Finally, for advice on actually selling your home, turn to "Handling Your Emotions When Selling Your Home" (page 154).

WHAT WILL THE HOUSE SELL FOR?

Consult an experienced local realtor to find out what comparable homes are currently selling for in your area. That way you can anticipate what you can expect to net from a sale. You may also benefit from getting an appraisal done, which will help to determine current market value (see "Get Appraised," page 186).

WHAT WILL IT COST TO MOVE AND LIVE ELSEWHERE?

As you negotiate your divorce settlement, account for your anticipated moving and new housing costs. What are your housing options where you live? Is it better and more affordable to buy a smaller, cheaper house or to rent? Are there rentals available where you live that meet your needs and are in the same school district?

Compare the cost of likely house payments (including any tax deductions for mortgage loan interest) with the anticipated rent for a similar place. Then also account for the costs associated with moving and/or storing items if you move into a smaller home.

 How to Handle Children Who Act Out

Many times, children can't put into words what they are feeling, so instead they put it into actions. In the midst of a stressful divorce, this can often result in some alarming behaviors.

Recently separated after a seven-year marriage, Kelley observed that her six-year-old daughter, Amanda, seemed more affected with the split than her three-year-old. With her dad not around, Amanda became aggressive and angry, and she complained of aches and pains in her body and of constant headaches. She also cut her hair twice. First, she snipped off a little, and then she chopped off a handful of hair. Kelley also noticed that Amanda was biting herself on her arms. She didn't know what to do to stop the troubling behaviors. Amanda's behavior was a sign that she was feeling stressed and overwhelmed by the changes in the family.

Depending on a child's age, stress from separation and divorce can show up differently. When his parents separated, fifteen-year-old Ryan reacted by withdrawing from his family and friends; he resorted to playing video games in his darkened room and began cutting class. Ryan numbed his feelings by experimenting with drugs and alcohol, and he fell in with the wrong crowd at school. His mom and dad were so busy fighting about the finances that they didn't realize Ryan was falling through the cracks until it was almost too late.

Some of what we know about children and divorce has been summarized as follows by Dr. Richard Niolon:

Effects of Parental Divorce on Children of Varying Ages		
AGE AT TIME OF DIVORCE	INITIAL REACTIONS	LATER REACTIONS (2 TO 10 YEARS)
Preschool (2.5 to 6 years)	Are much more likely to blame themselves for the divorce; also, likely to fear abandonment by the remaining parent. They may be confused, have fantasies about reconciliation, and show difficulties in expressing their feelings. Early studies showed that boys had more problems than girls, but later studies have not confirmed this; rather, boys and girls have different kinds of problems as a result of the divorce.	Are more likely to have fewer memories of either their own or their parents' earlier conflict; generally close to custodial parent and a competent stepparent. May feel anger at an unavailable noncustodial parent that prevents a strong adult relationship. *(continued on the next page)*

Effects of Parental Divorce on Children of Varying Ages (Continued)		
AGE AT TIME OF DIVORCE	INITIAL REACTIONS	LATER REACTIONS (2 TO 10 YEARS)
Elementary school (7 to 12 years)	Tend to express feelings of sadness, fear, and anger. They are less likely to blame themselves, but more likely to feel divided loyalties. They are better able to use extrafamilial support. There is some support for placing children with their same-sex parent for best adjustment.	Tend to have the most difficulties in adapting to stepparenting and remarriage; may challenge family rules and regulations, and throw back "You're not my real father/mother" during conflict. They tend to show decreased academic performance and disturbed peer relations.
Adolescence (13 to 18 years)	Show difficulty coping with anger, outrage, shame, and sadness. They are more likely to reexamine their own values, and may disengage from the family to do this.	Shares feelings of the 7 to 12 group but may not be able to express them. May fear long-term relationships with others, and show adjustment difficulties such as running away, truancy, and delinquency.

Source: Richard Niolon, PhD, "Children of Divorce and Adjustment," September 19, 2010, www.psychpage.com, accessed February 20, 2018. Used with permission.

If you have a child who is acting out, update their therapist on the child's behavior and seek the therapist's advice. Also, talk with your own therapist about your parenting style and how you handle conflict. These two areas greatly impact your children, and when addressed, they can make a big difference in how your children handle divorce.

Parenting Styles

Studies have shown that an authoritative style of parenting seems to help children adjust best during and after divorce. Despite its name, this doesn't reflect a harsh, cold, or unyielding manner. Rather, an authoritative style establishes and maintains reliable routines and enforces respectful behavior, while allowing for some individual decisions and flexibility. On the other hand, the permissive style of parenting is defined by having few behavioral guidelines and allowing children to make most personal decisions. Neither style refers to the emotional quality of the relationship, which should always be warm, open, and welcoming.

During a divorce, when parents provide and maintain a structure for their children, but still remain flexible, they provide stability and consistency. It's important to allow children to make some decisions on their own, and to express whatever they feel, while still maintaining parental control over the situation. This control, however, should not sacrifice emotional warmth. In general, research has found this to be the most effective parenting approach. Here are some ways to embody an authoritative parenting style effectively in the midst of a divorce.

ESTABLISH AND MAINTAIN ROUTINES

Stable events and schedules help children feel their world is predictable and dependable. Studies have found that maintaining the number of positive events in a child's life (for example, involvement in after-school activities) is crucial in predicting good adjustment after divorce. Contrary to popular opinion, increased recreational time (such as "Disneyland Dads" who splurge on fancy vacations) does not necessarily lead to better adjustment in children.

ALLOW CHILDREN TO MOVE BETWEEN
BOTH PARENTS' HOMES WITHOUT GUILT

Respect the fact that children are not wrong to visit and even love your ex. This means no dirty looks or conflict about parental visits. Remember, this is not about what your ex deserves, but showing respect for your children and helping them feel safe in a difficult situation. When this respectful behavior begins early on, children have an easier time connecting with the nonresidential parent.

REQUIRE RESPECT FOR FAMILY RULES AND VALUES

Establish a consistent bedtime, and make whatever rules you want about off-limit foods, television, and screen time. Then enforce those rules. All children test limits and will complain, but maintaining established boundaries reinforces the values they represent and creates a stable and dependable world for children.

ACKNOWLEDGE YOUR CHILDREN'S FEELINGS

Encourage children to express whatever they are feeling, and then just listen. Acknowledge, don't correct, what they say. Simply saying to your children, "I know it's hard not to have Daddy around," or "I bet you wish things could go back to the way they were," can help your children feel heard and understood. Reassure children that the divorce is not their fault and that it's okay to feel whatever they are feeling.

OFFER CHILDREN CHOICES TO PROVIDE
A SENSE OF PERSONAL CONTROL

Letting children make some personal decisions can help them have some sense of control about their lives when so much about a divorce is out of their control. However, keep these choices focused on everyday life, like what to eat, what to wear, or what movie to see. In general, avoid open-ended questions like "What do you want?"

These can become overwhelming, even on basic matters. Instead, present "this or that" decisions, like "Ponytail or headband?" "Oatmeal or scrambled eggs?" and so on.

MAKE TIME FOR CUDDLING AND FUN

During a divorce, make an effort to express affection, physically and verbally, every day with kids. Give a back rub at bedtime, put a love note in a lunch box, build Legos or have a tea party together, or go for a short walk after dinner. In these simple ways, you let children know, "I love you, and we're going to be okay."

Resolving Conflict

Children are always observing their parents for lessons in how to act in the world. This doesn't change during divorce, which is a great opportunity to show kids how to handle conflict well. It's helpful for children to see their parents resolve problems and disagreements and recover from angry exchanges, which almost can't be avoided during a divorce. Conversely, children will become upset and anxious if they witness their parents have frequent, angry, and conflicted exchanges that do not lead to resolution or peace. The worse the conflict — such as when parental fights get nasty and out of control, with name-calling, "kitchen sink" complaints, and dredging up buried resentments — the more harmful the impact.

If you struggle with handling conflict yourself, consider these steps for reducing it, resolving it, and minimizing its impact on your children:

EXPRESS YOUR NEEDS CLEARLY

When you need or want something, express that need clearly and without personal attacks. You do this by focusing on a single issue at a time, describing the details of what you need (just the facts), and refraining from making disparaging remarks about your ex-partner's character or behavior.

- **Do say:** "I'm going back to school in the fall. Child care will be $650 a month."
- **Don't say:** "I know you don't give a damn about who keeps the kids, but you're going to have to pay day-care expenses."

STATE YOUR FEELINGS USING "I" LANGUAGE

Own your feelings, no matter what you feel your spouse did to cause them. Take responsibility by saying "I feel," rather than seeking to blame by saying "You did this...." Avoid making assumptions, as well as below-the-belt comments to emotionally bash the other person into doing what you want.

- **Do say:** "I'm scared to think about how I'll come up with the money to pay for all of it."
- **Don't say:** "You're trying to punish me by making me beg you for money. You have to pay your part whether you like it or not."

FOCUS ON THE PRESENT, NOT THE PAST

Focus on the immediate situation, and don't bring up old feelings and hurts from the past. Raising the past often only escalates a situation, turning a small issue into a battle over, or a referendum on, your entire marriage.

- **Do say:** "We need to take Rachel to see a therapist to help her process how she's feeling since you got your own place."
- **Don't say:** "Rachel is going to be permanently screwed up and in therapy for the rest of her life because you left us for another woman."

BE WILLING TO BARGAIN OR COMPROMISE

Don't just demand. Consider your ex's perspective and what he might need or want. Consider making a request that includes what you are willing to offer in return. Good timing is sometimes everything.

- **Do say:** "I want you to pay half. Then, after I finish school and make more money, you can cut back on the child support you pay."
- **Don't say:** "You owe me $325 a month starting now."

PRACTICE AND REHEARSE

Try out what you plan to say. Ask someone to listen objectively and offer pointers on how to rephrase or clarify your request. Imagine any angry comments your spouse might throw at you and practice how you'll respond to him while remaining calm.

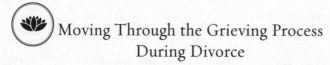 Moving Through the Grieving Process During Divorce

When you go through divorce, it's like a death of love. Even if you're the one who initiated the divorce, you will still grieve. This is because you are not only mourning the loss of your marriage, you are also grieving the loss of your hopes and dreams — the belief of what you thought your life was going to look like in this marriage.

You will experience all five stages of the grieving process, otherwise known as the Kübler-Ross model, during your divorce: denial, anger, bargaining, depression, and acceptance. People rarely move smoothly from one stage to the next. There is no beginning, middle, or end for each stage, and each stage might be visited several times. The ultimate goal is to get to the fifth stage: acceptance.

Some experts say it takes one year for every ten years of marriage to get over a divorce. In my experience, it can take longer. It took me five years — and I was married for sixteen. That's a long time. It may take you more or less time depending upon several factors, including who initiated the divorce, how happy you were in the marriage, and your own personal state of confidence and well-being.

So, as you manage your emotional recovery during divorce, give yourself a break. You will move through recovery at your own pace, angry one week, in denial the next.

As my clients experience the stages of grieving, I often see them engage in unmindful consumption, which only serves to aggravate the situation. This can show up as overeating, overshopping, over-drinking, or doing anything to excess to numb the pain. If this applies to you, understand and accept the five stages of grief and don't magnify problems with self-defeating behavior.

Here is my take on the five stages of grief during divorce.

Denial

This was my favorite. Drinking with girlfriends, shopping for things I didn't need, staying out late, and celebrating that I was SINGLE! Nothing like moving through a storm and pretending that everything is great. Denial is your psyche's way of protecting you from becoming emotionally overwhelmed. Denial is a useful coping mechanism, as long as it doesn't keep you from progressing to the next stage. Use this stage to your benefit, but don't abuse it. After a while, refusing to face reality becomes a problem.

It certainly did for Cathy. She had the rug pulled out from under her when her husband of twelve years filed for divorce and left her and their three young children for a younger woman. At first, Cathy dealt with her shock by partying with her girlfriends and going on a quest to meet a new, hot guy. After months of hard partying, however, Cathy was a mess. She had, among other things, become addicted to painkillers. When she faced her husband in court, she lost custody of her children because of her behavior. Don't be Cathy.

DATING DURING DIVORCE

After divorce, I always encourage women to jump back into the dating scene as soon as they feel ready. However, what about dating before the divorce is final? Especially when a divorce drags on and the marriage has already been "over" for quite a while, some women are tempted to start dating again. But this has some serious downsides, and in the end, dating before the divorce is final can negatively affect your case. It can cost you both emotionally and financially (especially when it comes to spousal support and living together), so it's a good idea to wait until you and your spouse are legally divorced before you start a new relationship. If you can't wait, you will need to be very discreet. Here are some reasons for caution:

- **The legal implications:** *Before you start dating, talk to your divorce lawyer to find out how it will affect your case. Depending upon the laws of your state, if you move in with your boyfriend, it can affect the way the marital property is divided, the spousal support payments you receive, and other aspects of your case.*

- **Your ex's reaction:** *Your ex might become uncooperative once he finds out you've started dating. He may not want to make any concessions during your divorce, and your divorce lawyer may have to fight for the things you're entitled to in court, which will increase the cost of your divorce and also increase the acrimony.*

- **The impact on children:** *If you have children, dating during divorce can be very problematic. They need you to focus your attention on them, not a new boyfriend. Children often feel threatened during a divorce, and adding a new person to the mix increases the confusion and their distress.*

- **Your romance:** *If your divorce isn't finalized, how well can you focus on a new romance? Is dating really the best thing for your own emotional well-being? How much easier and better will dating become once you've legally and emotionally put your marriage behind you?*

Anger

When your world is falling down around you, who better to blame for all your problems than a crazy ex-husband? If you get a flat tire, the washing machine breaks, or the internet isn't working, it's his fault. Perhaps because you feel that your ex (or life) has treated you unfairly, you have no role in any adversity that comes your way.

During the anger phase, your husband will become the worst lover you ever had, ugly beyond description, a slob, a wimp...your anger will do a number on him and his character. My advice about the anger stage? Have at it! As long as there are no little ears to hear your disparaging and insulting remarks about your ex, feel free to let out all the pent-up anger you stuffed during the denial stage. Your therapist and girlfriends are your allies here.

Bargaining

In this stage, you attempt to repair and undo the damage done to your life. Bargaining is when you stop and say, "I can't handle this emotionally. I'll accept anything, but I can't go through with this divorce."

Bargaining attempts to put on the brakes, to stop that runaway train and get your "old life" back. It might not have been a great life, but it was a lot better than the chaos and uncertainty you are experiencing now. During the bargaining stage, your ex will be the best lover you ever had. You will miss his beautiful face and his manly demeanor. He was God's gift and you want him back. You need to quickly move through the bargaining stage.

Bargaining is a last-ditch attempt to come to terms with the decision to divorce. If you made the decision to leave, you may convince yourself that you made a mistake.

If you were left, you may begin to pursue your husband and woo him back at all costs to you and your self-esteem. Just remember, both spouses will go through the bargaining stage. When this happens at the same time, couples who should get divorced sometimes reconcile and get back together. Then, approximately two years later, I often get a phone call that the reconciliation didn't work and the woman is ready to pull the trigger.

Depression

You'll be in bed or in front of the television for most of this stage. Sadness, sometimes debilitating sadness, becomes your constant companion. This is the one stage we all expect. We know that depression is going to hit. What we don't realize is that depression can go hand-in-hand with *all* the stages of grief. You may not bathe for three days during the denial stage. Hair care might take a back seat during the anger stage. And when flat-out depressed? You may open a can of SpaghettiOs or a box of cereal for your kids for dinner — something you never thought you would do.

During divorce, it is easy to become despondent and stuck. When this happens, addictive behavior can take over and hold you back. It is critical that you fight the urge to retreat; ask your support network of family and friends for help. You must also regularly seek the help of your therapist when you feel depressed.

When I was depressed during my divorce, I found that focusing on where the love is — in my case, my children — got me through. That and doubling-down on my mindfulness practice. These things lifted me out of the depression that I experienced during the "dark night of the soul" that often accompanies divorce.

Acceptance

Finally. When it hits you, you'll throw your head back and laugh. There is light at the end of the tunnel and life ahead. You've moved through adversity and learned from it. Full steam ahead!

Be warned, though. Acceptance doesn't mean you won't still experience negative emotions about your divorce. You may still feel anger and sadness at the loss of your marriage, and negative emotions can hijack you years later, when you least expect it. What acceptance means is that you've learned to "accept" the reality of the situation. You may always have feelings of regret over the loss of your marriage, but you accept that price. You know you did the right thing and are no longer stuck in the grief. If there are still feelings of grief, they are at least no longer holding you back from living life.

Mindful Action Steps

- Keep up your therapy appointments. While the support of family and friends goes a long way, there is no substitute for expert advice as you navigate the stages of grieving that accompany divorce.
- Cry it out so you can eliminate those toxic emotions.
- Double-down on your mindfulness practice (see chapter 1).
- Write honestly in your journal about any addictive behaviors that are taking hold.
- If you are stuck in depression or self-medicating, consult your therapist about seeking an evaluation to determine whether short-term use of antidepressants may be helpful.

CHAPTER 5

Getting What You Need

"If one advances confidently in the direction of [her] dreams, and endeavors to live the life [she] has imagined, [she] will meet with a success unimagined in common hours."

— Henry David Thoreau

*H*ow do you get what you need in your divorce if your husband is the primary breadwinner in the family and controls the finances? This chapter outlines how to get what you need and make your husband pay for it. Yes. That's right. Your husband will likely have to pay the bill if he is the primary wage earner in the family.

This is true in even the direst circumstances, as Emily's story shows. On Christmas Eve, Emily found a receipt from a jewelry store on the floor of the walk-in closet that she shared with her husband, David. At first, Emily was thrilled when she found the receipt for over $500 from an expensive jewelry boutique in town. She assumed that David, who had been distant and cold for some time, was going to surprise her Christmas morning with something wonderful and that their marriage would get back on track. Christmas morning arrived, the three kids opened their gifts, and then Emily's husband pulled out his gift for her — a new doorbell.

At first, Emily thought the doorbell was a joke. But when no bracelet or earrings were forthcoming, she realized the truth: The expensive jewelry was intended for someone else. As she sat in front of the tree, tears streaming down her face, Emily knew what she had to do, but she had no idea how she was going to get what she needed, since she was a stay-at-home mom and David controlled the finances.

Emily arrived in my office in shock, but we were able to obtain child and spousal support for her and the children, as well as a court order that David pay Emily's attorney fees so that Emily could move forward and rebuild her life.

DIVORCE HACKS

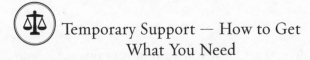 ## Temporary Support — How to Get What You Need

Temporary spousal support is a form of alimony or "maintenance" paid by one spouse to the other during the divorce process. *Temporary child support* is paid by one spouse to the other for the support of the children. A court will usually award the lower-earning spouse enough support to meet basic needs while the divorce is proceeding. Essentially, temporary support allows the spouses to maintain the marital standard of living — or something close to it — even though they're now living separately. But keep in mind, since you and your spouse are setting up two households on the same income you had been using to run one household, you may each experience a dip in your standard of living, at least initially.

If you can't cover your own expenses during your divorce, you'll need to file a request for temporary support, since it is not automatic. Specifically, you'll need to file a written motion, or "petition," which explains why you're entitled to temporary support. You'll also need to produce evidence to support your request, which may include your pay stubs, bank records, credit card bills, rent or mortgage payments, utility bills, student loan balances, medical bills, and children's expenses — basically, any documents that show your current income and expenses. This is what I guided you to prepare in chapter 4 (see "Preparing Your Financial Disclosures," page 92), and you will use this now in your request for support.

Don't wait to do this. Charlene's case (from chapter 1) is illustrative. After participating in the "collaborative process" for six years, she requested that her husband, Richard, reimburse her for her and the children's living expenses. She'd spent her inheritance to keep the house and pay the bills while the collaborative process was under way. Even though Richard earned well over a million dollars a year and had the means to reimburse her, he refused. And since Charlene had not filed a request for temporary support at the start, she missed her opportunity.

Qualifying for Temporary Support

Spousal and child support is a matter of state law, and the rules vary a bit depending on where you live. In California and many states, the court uses a "guideline" calculator, such as the DissoMaster, to calculate temporary support. This program uses each party's respective income, the amount of time spent with the children, and several other factors (health insurance, mortgage interest, property taxes) to determine temporary support. Most state laws require a judge to look at all or some of the following factors when deciding whether a temporary support award is appropriate:

- Each spouse's financial condition
- The requesting spouse's need for support
- The paying spouse's ability to pay for support
- Each spouse's age and health
- Each spouse's employability and work experience
- Each spouse's ability to work
- In some states, each spouse's potential fault for causing the divorce

While a court may consider several factors, the most important factors when deciding whether temporary spousal support is necessary are the requesting spouse's financial needs and the paying spouse's financial condition or ability to pay support.

The recipient spouse's need

If you're requesting temporary support, you'll need to prove that you can't meet your most basic living expenses on your own. For example, if you and your spouse earn similar incomes, a court probably won't award you temporary support. In contrast, if you have significant student loan debts, no job, and mounting medical bills, you will need temporary spousal support. But even if you have demonstrated a financial need, a court won't order temporary maintenance unless your spouse has the ability to support you.

Your spouse's ability to pay support

A court will award temporary spousal support only if the earning spouse can pay. This means the paying spouse needs to earn enough money to cover basic expenses and contribute something to the requesting spouse. For example, a court won't order temporary support if it would require the paying spouse to forgo groceries, health insurance, or a car payment.

A judge will usually require both spouses to complete financial disclosures (see "Preparing Your Financial Disclosures," page 92), which detail each spouse's assets, debts, and monthly sources of income and expenses. Your spouse's regular salary, overtime pay, bonuses, and Social Security benefits will be evaluated to determine whether a temporary support award is appropriate in your case.

Impact of the parenting plan on child support

In making the child support determination, one of the factors courts consider is the percentage of time the children spend with each parent. Courts typically use a support calculator to determine temporary support, and the "time-share" (percentage of time the children spend with each parent) is plugged into the calculation. How to obtain the parenting plan you want is addressed below in "Parenting Plan — Making a Parenting Plan That Works for You and Your Kids" (page 144).

(page 144)

Sylvia learned the hard way about how time-share can affect child support. When she and her husband, Lance, separated, Lance

> **INSIDER TIP**
> *Divorcing dads often try to maximize their time with the children in an effort to reduce the child support they will be ordered to pay. Watch out for this trap!*

convinced their teenage son, Jack, to live with him. When Jack moved in with his dad, he was surprised to find girls' toiletries in the bathroom. His dad explained that his girlfriend and her daughter were living with him and that Jack would be sharing a bathroom with the daughter. When Jack expressed surprise and disappointment that his dad hadn't told him this before he agreed to move in, Lance said, "Well, I don't want to pay your mother child support."

WILL MY TEMPORARY SUPPORT AWARD BECOME PERMANENT?

Temporary support awards end as soon as your divorce becomes final. You may or may not be entitled to alimony once you're divorced. The factors used to decide if alimony is appropriate aren't the same as the factors on which a temporary support order is based. Specifically, temporary support usually helps needy spouses get back on their feet. A judge will typically award permanent support or maintenance when there's a great disparity in wealth between the two spouses, one spouse is disabled or unable to work, it was a long-term marriage, or there's some other factor that justifies permanent support.

Requesting Temporary Support

To request temporary spousal or child support, your attorney will file a motion and the court will set a hearing to evaluate whether you are entitled to receive support. Your lawyer will work with you to prepare the documents that will be filed with the court. Typically, you will submit a statement or declaration, usually prepared under oath, about why you need support along with your financial declaration (see chapter 4). Be aware that in some jurisdictions, such as in California, it can take four to six weeks from the time you file your request for your matter to be heard by a judge. This document should include the following information:

- Describe your husband's education, his work history, and his earnings. Use tax returns to show what he has traditionally earned. This is effective if he is claiming to be earning less now.
- List your education, work history, and earnings. If you have experienced any illnesses or handicaps that have precluded you from working, describe these.
- List any time you have taken off work to raise children or to support your husband.
- Include your financial disclosures setting forth your household expenses. This is important evidence that quantifies your need.

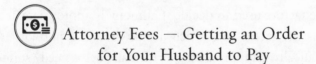

Attorney Fees — Getting an Order for Your Husband to Pay

Contested divorces can be very expensive propositions. With spouses arguing over everything from alimony and child support to who gets custody of the family pet, attorney fees can skyrocket quickly. In fact, those monthly legal invoices are what finally cause many couples to hunker down, put animosity aside, and try to peaceably resolve their differences. Often, one spouse will ask the other to pay both sides' divorce-related legal fees. How successful that will be depends on the particular facts of your case.

However, there are two main circumstances when one spouse

may be required to pay some or all of the other spouse's attorney's fees:

- **A large income disparity:** If your spouse earns far more than you do, ask your attorney whether you qualify for an attorney fee order under the laws of your state.
- **Misconduct and bad behavior:** If your spouse is deliberately driving up costs by causing delays, filing frivolous motions, or failing to abide by court orders, ask your attorney whether you qualify for attorney fees as a sanction.

A Large Income Disparity

In most states, particularly when there is a large income gap between spouses, family law courts and judges are authorized to order the higher-earning spouse to cover some or all of the lower-earning (or nonearning) spouse's attorney's fees.

For example, in New Jersey, courts will order an award of attorney fees to a lower-earning spouse — often because it's clear the higher-earning spouse will be able to recover financially after the divorce is finalized.

In some states, like California, the policy underlying attorney fee awards is that if one spouse can afford to pay for both sides' fees, while the other spouse would have to proceed without a lawyer absent some contribution, then an order for fees will be considered both necessary and fair, in order to "level the legal playing field" between the parties.

But in situations where neither spouse is making a sizable income, yet there's still an earnings difference, decisions on attorney fees are more likely to vary from state to state. For example, in New Jersey, courts aren't likely to grant a request for attorney fees if the lower-earning spouse will at some point have access to marital assets that can be used to generate sufficient funds to pay those fees. This might include:

- bank accounts
- stocks
- a 401K retirement plan

If a cash-poor spouse needs money up front for a lawyer, the court may also let the spouse use some of the shared marital property for their attorney's fees, with the understanding that when marital property is eventually divided, the other spouse will be reimbursed. For example, the proceeds from the sale of a family home may be placed in a joint two-signature account, and the court may order that attorney fees will be paid directly from that account, subject to reallocation when the divorce is finalized.

> **INSIDER TIP**
> *When one spouse intentionally disrupts the court process and drives up the cost of litigation, a judge might be inclined to grant the other spouse's request for attorney fees as a penalty for that conduct.*

Misconduct and Bad Behavior

Judges don't like it when spouses behave badly during the divorce process. Not only does bad behavior drive up attorney fees (for both sides), it prolongs the divorce process, causes unnecessary stress, and wastes valuable court time and resources.

Some common examples of disruptive tactics include the following:

- Constantly filing motions (formal requests) with the court about trivial matters.
- Refusing to comply with court orders (usually until threatened with contempt of court).
- Delaying providing requested information to the other spouse (such as financial documents).
- Failing to appear for hearings or court-ordered mediation sessions.

If your spouse (or, possibly, his lawyer) engages in this type of behavior, it will invariably drive up your own attorney's fees. Your lawyer will have to respond to the frivolous motions, file their own motions to force compliance with court orders, and keep going back to court for rescheduled hearings.

If your spouse is disrupting the court process to drive up the cost of litigation, a judge may order him to pay some — if not all — of your attorney's fees. A court may determine that it's simply not fair for you to pay for your spouse's behavior.

Two-Income Households

When dual-income spouses divorce, it's becoming increasingly unusual for judges to issue orders requiring one spouse to pay the other's attorney's fees. Today, it's less likely that one spouse is completely reliant on the other for money. When faced with spouses who each earn about the same income, courts are generally inclined to let spouses bear the burden of their own attorney's fees.

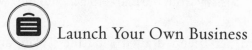 Launch Your Own Business

The smartest and happiest divorced women come to terms with the same essential truth that starts this book: You cannot rely on your ex-husband as your long-term financial solution, nor on "finding another man." The only person you can rely on is yourself, and unless you're extremely wealthy, your economic level will decrease after divorce. The same income that was used to run one household is now running two. These are the facts — but they are not obstacles to happiness.

You can choose to use this opportunity to increase your earnings through your own means. And if you do, you may discover that you are far more capable of achieving greatness than you ever knew. In chapter 2, I suggest that you brainstorm a potential new business and lay the groundwork while the divorce process is just starting (see "Be Your Own Boss," page 51). Now, before your divorce is finalized, I suggest putting your ideas on paper and formulating a business plan. Get specific about what your potential business will need, since that can influence what you ask for in your divorce settlement. In other words, this is the time to plan so that when your divorce is finalized, you can go for it! In this computer-driven age, all you need is an idea and serious drive to start a business, and many single women are becoming entrepreneurs. You can do this, too, not only providing for yourself, but doing it on your terms.

Madeline could see all the red flags that her marriage was beyond repair. While she was still married and before her divorce was finalized, she began brainstorming about a new business with a friend and respected colleague. She had years of experience in sales and marketing, but she wanted the freedom that having her own business would afford. Together, Madeline and her friend conceived an idea for an app that would allow consumers to explore and book beauty, fitness, and wellness services anytime, anywhere. The app was something both Madeline and her friend felt they would use themselves, it was missing from the marketplace, and they were passionate about it.

Madeline and her friend drafted a business plan, and from this they created a fifteen-page "pitch deck," which is a succinct, PowerPoint-style presentation that's used to obtain funding. They also searched out like-minded entrepreneurs — using the online service Meetup (www.meetup.com) — and started sharing their idea. Through Meetup, they found a mentor who helped them tune up their pitch deck until they were ready to pitch their idea. They shared their plan with former business colleagues and anyone they thought could be helpful. One person, the head of an IT company, liked the idea so much that he asked to be part of it. He became their third cofounder and supplied the debt financing. By the time Madeline's divorce was final, her business was ready to go.

This section briefly outlines the major steps for launching a business. This starts with making a business plan and defining the market, and it includes deciding how to fund the business, securing that funding, taking a series of legal steps, and getting the word out.

Create a Business Plan

A business plan is an essential road map for business success. This living document describes every aspect of the proposed business, and it generally projects three to five years ahead, outlining the route a company intends to take to grow revenues. Banks and lenders often require a business plan before they will provide funding. Angel investors will expect it in your pitch. However, a business plan is much more than a fund-raising tool. It's your blueprint for how you will put your business together.

Below is a list of the traditional elements of a business plan and what each includes.

- **Executive summary:** Your executive summary is a snapshot of your business plan as a whole and touches on your company profile and goals.
- **Company description:** Your company description provides information on what you do, what differentiates your business from others, and the markets your business serves.
- **Market analysis:** Before launching your business, it is essential for you to research your business industry, the market, and your competitors. (See more on this below.)
- **Organization and management:** Every business is structured differently. This describes yours. If you need, ask for advice about the best organization and management structure for your business.
- **Service or product line:** What do you sell? How does it benefit your customers? What is the product life cycle? As necessary, get tips on how to tell the story about your product or service.
- **Marketing and sales:** How do you plan to market your business? What is your sales strategy? See "How to Use

Social Media to Increase Your Business" (page 236) for more advice.

- **Funding request:** If you are seeking funding for your business, find out about the necessary information you should include in your plan. What does the bank or institution you're approaching need? (See below for more on how to finance a business and how to pitch to investors.)
- **Financial projections:** If you need funding, it's critical to provide financial projections to back up your request. You want to show that the business will make a profit.
- **Appendix:** An appendix is optional, but it's a useful place to include information such as résumés, permits, and leases.

Know Your Market and Target Audience

Find out whether people will actually buy your product or service. This may be the most important thing you do. You can do this by validating your market. In other words, who, exactly, will buy your product or service other than your family or friends? (And don't say, "Everyone in America will want my product!" Trust me — they won't.) What is the size of your target market? Who are your customers? Is your product or service relevant to their everyday life? Why do they need it?

In your business plan, you want to define and quantify your market and target audience with as many specific numbers and as much factual data as possible. Research online the relevant industry associations, which often provide this kind of market data for free. Read industry articles related to your product or service, and quantify the demographics of your market with census data. However, the most important way to get this information is to ask potential customers directly and listen to what they say. Who is most interested in your product or service and why?

Funding Your Business

Unless you are independently wealthy, financing a new business usually involves a combination of options, including loans, grants, venture capital, and government-financing programs for starting or expanding a small business. Whatever works best in your situation, especially when applying for a traditional bank loan, you will need a solid business plan in order to obtain funding.

The kind of financing you will need depends in part on the type of business you might build — a lifestyle business (smaller amount of start-up funds), a franchise (moderate investment depending on the franchise), or a high-tech business (significant capital investment). The better you understand the nature of your business, the better you will understand the amount of money and the kind of funding you need to launch and grow your business.

This book can't provide all the financial advice you need, so I recommend exploring the Small Business Administration (SBA, www.sba.gov), which provides resources to help women entrepreneurs launch new businesses, grow their businesses, and compete in the global marketplace. SBA provides online resources, financing opportunities, and Women's Business Centers to help you succeed. Take advantage of their free training and counseling services, which range from preparing a business plan and securing financing to expanding an existing business.

For women going through a divorce, understanding what funding their future business will require can inform their settlement negotiations. For example, you may decide to sell the family home to obtain cash to invest in your new venture. Or you may negotiate to obtain a cash equalization rather than wait for disbursement of retirement funds. Once you know what personal resources you'll have postdivorce, you can approach banks, angel investors, and venture capitalists to help you raise the rest.

What is an angel investor?

Funding a start-up business can be a confounding process. For instance, who are angel investors and venture capitalists, what do they do, and how do you find them? In short, they are individuals and companies who make investments directly into private companies. If you can't or would rather not take out a bank loan, then finding one of these types of investors may be critical.

Angel investors are individuals, often successful businesspeople, who invest their own personal funds in what they consider to be potentially rewarding business opportunities. Angel investors can also be groups formed through investor pools and crowdfunding. Because they invest their own funds, factors such as confidence, trustworthiness, and delivery play a significant role in their decisions to invest. In general, for a business that's just starting, angel investors are the most likely source of funding (in addition to loans).

Here are the main characteristics of angel investors:

- An individual investor
- Often willing to make riskier investments in early-stage or start-up businesses
- Also invest in established companies
- Have experience and contacts to contribute
- May be willing to be "hands-off" in terms of running the business
- May be willing to be "hands-on" and add important skills

What is a venture capitalist?

Venture capitalists run firms or companies that use other people's money to invest in established businesses with a high potential for growth. A venture capital company raises money from others who are interested in investing, and they use that communal fund to buy shares in private companies. Typically, venture capital firms invest during a later stage of a business's growth, when the concept is proven, the potential for profit is clear, and all that's needed is more cash for the business to quickly expand.

Here are the main features of venture capital firms:

- A company or business rather than an individual
- Seldom fund start-ups, unless there's a compelling reason (for example, previously successful founders in high-profit fields)
- Have industry contacts
- Require a seat on the board of the funded business

How to meet angel investors

Madeline was lucky enough to find an investor through her professional network, and that's the first place to look. However, you can find angel investors in other ways, though pitching your idea is not always straightforward. Here is a list of ways to seek angel investors:

- **At events related to your industry:** Industry events are a great way to meet angel investors, who are often on the prowl looking for promising start-ups.
- **In online platforms:** You can find online, directory-style websites that help you connect globally with angel investors. You can then set up pitch meetings with potential investors in your area. Some of these websites include Gust (www.gust.com), Angel Investment Network (www.angelinvestmentnetwork.us), and US Angel Investors (www.usangelinvestors.com).
- **At angel-investor events:** Angel investors (and venture capitalists) hold events year-round all across the country. These give you the opportunity to pitch your idea, not to one, but to hundreds of angel investors looking for promising start-ups and entrepreneurs. Check out Startup Grind (www.startupgrind.com).
- **At angel-investment networks and groups:** You may also contact an angel investor, investment network, or

angel investor group directly to pitch them your idea. This may seem like the simplest way to meet an angel investor, but it's also the least effective. Angel investors usually screen ideas before even looking at them, and unless you have a connection or advocate with an individual or in a network, your contact request will probably be lost in the thousands they receive each day.

CONSIDER HIRING A FUND-RAISING ADVISER

If you are not confident in your fund-raising skills, you can always employ fund-raising advisers to help you get your start-up rolling. Similar to investors themselves, fund-raising advisers will only take on clients whose businesses have high potential (and so will appeal to investors), so make sure you prepare a great presentation for them, too.

How to Pitch to Angel Investors

Whether you are meeting with an angel investor, a venture capitalist, or a bank to secure a loan, you have to prepare a presentation to pitch your idea. This is particularly important with angel investors, who pay close attention to the quality of your pitch. So make sure you lay the groundwork for an excellent delivery by doing the following:

- **Connect effectively before your meeting:** Angel investors will want to contact you and ask questions even before your meeting if they really like your start-up idea. Giving them open communication channels can cultivate your relationship, which can be a huge deciding factor.
- **Within companies, enlist a vocal champion:** If you want to approach an investor group, try to recruit a vocal champion inside of the group before you make your pitch. Or recruit someone who is close to the individual investor. Having a vocal champion gives you credibility,

and this can make all the difference in convincing investors to even consider the pros and cons of your start-up.

- **Research investors and know their process:** Each individual or group of angel investors follows a unique process to choosing a start-up. Familiarize yourself with this process, and use the information to deliver what they want.

DELIVER A MEMORABLE PRESENTATION

To convince investors to fund your business, you need to do more than simply hand them your business plan. You need to sell it. You use the information in your business plan to create your pitch, and the biggest, most prominent element of your pitch is delivering a strong presentation, one that is confident, knowledgeable, and dramatic. Like Madeline, you might consider crafting a "pitch deck" or slide presentation that succinctly summarizes your business (look online for examples used by other companies). Whether you use slides, samples, props, or just talk, a great pitch does the following things:

- **Tells a compelling story:** Remember, your potential investors are not customers, so tailor your presentation to achieve maximum engagement.
- **Gets straight to the point:** Presentations have designated time slots, usually between ten and fifteen minutes. Stick to your allotted slot to show you respect the angel investor's time.
- **Covers the money:** Angel investors may be swayed by emotion, but they are still investors. Don't be afraid to cover the financial aspects and exit options in case your start-up does not generate revenue.
- **Answers all questions:** At the end of your presentation, investors will bombard you with questions, so make

sure you are ready to answer anything from finances to operations.

- **Is polished and persuasive:** Employ strong public speaking skills to deliver an eloquent presentation. This includes tone of voice, body language, effective visual aids, and so on. Practice your pitch.
- **Aims to build a relationship, not to close a sale:** Don't treat your meeting as a sales opportunity. View it as a chance to cultivate a good relationship and establish rapport with your potential investors.

Get Your Legal Ducks in a Row

No matter how busy things get, set aside some time to address these legal matters. Get your legal ducks in a row right from the start, which will help you avoid any pitfalls down the road as your business grows.

CONFIRM THE LEGALITY OF YOUR BUSINESS NAME

Before you start printing out business cards, make sure the great new name you thought of isn't infringing on the rights of an already existing business. In most cases, you don't need an attorney for this task because you can perform a free search online to check all business names registered in your state. Then, take your search to the next level and conduct a free trademark search to see if your name is available for use in all fifty states.

REGISTER YOUR BUSINESS NAME OR DBA

A DBA ("doing business as") must be filed whenever you do business under a different name. If you've got a sole proprietorship or general partnership, a DBA is needed if your company name is different than your own name. For an LLC or corporation, a DBA must be filed to conduct business using a name that's different than the official corporation or LLC name you filed. For example, if your company is officially incorporated as JobNet, Inc., you will need to file DBAs for the variations JobNet.com and JobNet. These are typically filed at the state and/or county level.

INCORPORATE YOUR BUSINESS OR FORM AN LLC

Forming an LLC (limited liability company) or corporation is an essential step to protect your personal assets (such as your personal property or your child's college fund) from any liabilities of the company. Each business structure has its advantages and disadvantages, depending on your specific circumstances. Three popular options are an LLC (great for small businesses that want legal protection, but minimal formality), an S Corporation (great for small businesses that can qualify), or a C Corporation (for companies who plan to seek funding from a venture capitalist or go public).

GET A FEDERAL TAX ID NUMBER

To distinguish your business as a separate legal entity from yourself, you'll need to obtain a federal tax identification number, also referred to as an employer identification number (EIN). Issued by the IRS, the tax ID number is similar to your personal Social Security number and allows the IRS to track your company's transactions. If you're a sole proprietor, you're not obligated to get a tax ID number, but it's still good practice, as you won't have to provide your personal Social Security number for business matters.

LEARN ABOUT EMPLOYEE LAWS

Your legal obligations as an employer begin as soon as you hire your first employee. You should spend time with an employment law professional to fully understand your obligations for these (and other) procedures: federal and state payroll and withholding taxes, self-employment taxes, antidiscrimination laws, OSHA regulations, unemployment insurance, workers' compensation rules, and wage and hour requirements.

OBTAIN THE NECESSARY BUSINESS PERMITS AND LICENSES

Depending on your business type and physical location, you may be required to have one or more business licenses or permits at the state, local, or even federal level. Such licenses include a general business operation license, zoning and land-use permits, sales tax license, health department permits, and occupational or professional licenses.

FILE FOR TRADEMARK PROTECTION

You're not actually required by law to register a trademark. Using a name instantly gives you common-law rights as an owner, even without formal registration. However, as expected, trademark law is complex, and simply registering a DBA in your state doesn't automatically give you common-law rights. In order to claim first use, the name has to be "trademarkable" and in use in commerce.

Since you've spent untold hours brainstorming the ideal name, and you'll be putting even more effort into cultivating name recognition, you should consider registering your trademark for proper legal protection. Registering a trademark makes it exponentially easier to recover your properties, like if someone happens to use your company name as their Twitter handle. Having the right documentation means you have the legal right to that handle, and Twitter will take steps to give it to you.

OPEN A BANK ACCOUNT TO START BUILDING BUSINESS CREDIT

When you rely on your personal credit to fund your business, your personal mortgage, auto loan, and personal credit cards all affect your ability to qualify for a business loan (and for how much). Using business credit separates your personal activities from that of the business. To begin building your business credit, you should open a bank account in the name of your company, and the account should show a cash flow capable of taking on a business loan.

Build a Support Network and Get the Word Out

You will need to cultivate a network of supporters, advisers, partners, allies, and vendors when it comes time to launch and grow your business. Lay the groundwork now and start networking locally, nationally, and via social networks. Join networks like International Association of Women (IAW, www.iawomen.com), which has more than 850,000 accomplished women members from varying backgrounds and fields. You can network online and in person through IAW. You can also network through your local chamber of commerce or other relevant business groups. Here are some networking basics:

- When attending networking events, ask others what they do, and think about how you can help them. The key is to listen more to others than to yourself.
- No matter what group you join, be generous, help others, and make introductions without charging them.
- By becoming a generous leader, you will be the first person that comes to mind when someone you've helped needs your service or hears of someone else who needs your service.

Finally, to broadcast your business, you will need to embrace and use the most effective online tools (Twitter, Facebook, YouTube, LinkedIn). Become facile with social media now, if you aren't already, for the purpose of promoting your business. You can use social networks as "pointer" sites; that is, to point to anything you think will be of interest to create fans and followers who will be potential clients and referral sources. For more on this, see "How to Use Social Media to Increase Your Business" (page 236).

Even though social networks are essential in today's marketplace, don't underestimate the power of other methods to get the word out: word-of-mouth marketing, website and internet marketing tools, public relations, blog posts, columns and articles, speeches, email, and newsletters.

Parenting Plan — Making a Parenting Plan
That Works for You and Your Kids

A parenting plan or custody agreement outlines how you and your children's father will continue to care and provide for your children after you separate. Most courts require you to attempt to work out a parenting plan before your case is heard. If you cannot agree on a plan, the judge will order what it will be. Since the judge can't know all the nuances of your and your children's needs, you're better off working out a plan with your ex rather than relying on the judge to sort it out. An effective plan is personalized to fit the needs of your family situation, and it specifies every aspect of the shared parenting arrangement, including parenting schedules, communication, finances, child care, schools, and so on.

In chapter 6, I discuss strategies for negotiating the parenting plan in order to reach a settlement (see page 183). In this chapter, I discuss the aspects that the plan should cover. As you consider all the topics below, here are some questions to keep in mind:

- What child-care responsibilities did each parent have before the separation?
- What involvement does each parent want in the child's recreational and extracurricular activities?
- What are the individual needs and important issues for each of your children?
- What are the parenting strengths of each parent?
- How do the parents want to share parenting responsibilities?
- What type of relationship do your children have with one another, and do children need individual time with each parent?
- What do your children prefer?
- How will you and the other parent put your children's needs above your own?

- How will you and the other parent protect your children from conflict and disagreements between the parents?
- How will you tell your children the details of your parenting plan?

Legal Custody, Physical Custody, and Visitation

Your plan must designate who has legal custody and the authority to make decisions for and about your children. Joint legal custody means that both parents share decision-making about the health, welfare, and safety of the children. Joint legal custody is the default, unless there is a valid reason that one parent is unfit (such as drug or alcohol abuse, neglect, or mental illness). In exercising joint legal custody, it is required that the parties are in agreement in making decisions on the following matters for the minor children:

- Enrollment in, or termination of, attendance at a particular private or public school
- Participation in particular religious activities or institutions
- Beginning or ending of psychiatric, psychological, or other mental health counseling or therapy including, but not limited to, educational testing
- Selection or change of a doctor, dentist, or other health professional (except in emergency situations)
- Routine medical checkups and nonemergency medical, dental, and other elective care treatment
- Permission for tattoos, piercings, and all other permanent alterations of the minor children's bodies
- A passport application or issuance of a passport

Physical custody is distinct from legal custody and refers to the parent the children spend the most time with. Even if both parents share joint legal custody, one parent might be granted sole physical custody, so that children live with or spend the most time with that parent. The other spouse would be awarded "visitation." This would be some lesser, unequal share of time with the children. Courts typically order the status quo when it comes to physical visitation. For example, in a traditional arrangement where the father is the breadwinner and the mother is a homemaker, the court might order an 80/20 time-share arrangement — where the mother has the children 80 percent of the time and the father has them 20 percent of the time. As an example, this might translate into a schedule where the father has visitation every other weekend and Thursday nights. Courts used to routinely order that mothers had children most of the time, and fathers had visitation, but that has changed. Courts are now much more apt to order a 50/50 time-share arrangement, especially if both parents are employed. Those types of schedules are discussed below.

Parenting Schedule

Typically, there are three types of parenting schedules divorcing couples adopt when they agree to a 50/50 split of time with the kids: the 2-2-3 schedule, the 2-2-5-5 schedule, and alternating weeks. The pattern that these schedules follow is to divide either one-week or two-week time periods equally between the parents. Then the cycle simply repeats throughout the year. However, you can set up anything that works for you. For instance, you might want the children to sleep mainly with one parent, so the other parent takes them after school and on Friday night. Use these schedules as a starting place and adjust them to fit your needs. The beauty of working this out with your spouse is that you can be flexible and agree to uneven times and arrange handoffs that suit your schedules and the kids.

THE 2-2-3 SCHEDULE

Very young children typically do better with fewer days away from Mom. I often see a 2-2-3 schedule for children under the age of five if both parents work.

In this custody schedule, one parent has the child for two days, the other parent has the child for the next two days, and then the child goes back to the first parent for a three-day weekend. It ends up working out that each parent has two days with the child during the week and the parents alternate with a long weekend. Here is a calendar view to make it clear.

JANUARY 2018

SUNDAY	MONDAY	TUESDAY	WEDNESDAY	THURSDAY	FRIDAY	SATURDAY
31	3:00 PM 1	2	3:00 PM 3	4	3:00 PM 5	6
7	3:00 PM 8	9	3:00 PM 10	11	3:00 PM 12	13
14	3:00 PM 15	16	3:00 PM 17	18	3:00 PM 19	20
21	3:00 PM 22	23	3:00 PM 24	25	3:00 PM 26	27
28	3:00 PM 29	30	3:00 PM 31	1	3:00 PM 2	3

You can see with this schedule that the parents have an equal amount of time with the children. There is more switching back and forth than a 2-2-5-5 custody schedule (below). If the parents live close by, and children do all right with the changes, then this arrangement can work very well.

THE 2-2-5-5 SCHEDULE

A 2-2-5-5 schedule divides the children's time equally between the parents, but there is less switching back and forth than the 2-2-3 schedule. In the 2-2-5-5 schedule, children live two days with one parent, two days with the other parent, five days with the first parent, and five days with the second parent. The children spend more time away from each parent, but this schedule can work quite well for children who are in school. It looks like this:

JANUARY 2018

SUNDAY	MONDAY	TUESDAY	WEDNESDAY	THURSDAY	FRIDAY	SATURDAY
31	1	2	3:00 PM 3	4	5	6
7	3:00 PM 8	9	3:00 PM 10	11	3:00 PM 12	13
14	15	16	3:00 PM 17	18	19	20
21	3:00 PM 22	23	3:00 PM 24	25	3:00 PM 26	27
28	29	30	3:00 PM 31	1	2	3

THE ALTERNATING WEEKS SCHEDULE

The alternating weeks schedule is a 50/50 residential schedule. Your children spend one week with one parent, and the next week with the other parent. This repeats throughout the year. Here's how this schedule looks in the calendar.

JANUARY 2018

SUNDAY	MONDAY	TUESDAY	WEDNESDAY	THURSDAY	FRIDAY	SATURDAY
31	1	2	3	4	3:00 PM 5	6
7	8	9	10	11	3:00 PM 12	13
14	15	16	17	18	3:00 PM 19	20
21	22	23	24	25	3:00 PM 26	27
28	29	30	31	1	3:00 PM 2	3

Older children can typically handle longer periods of time away from a parent. The alternating week schedule can work well for teenagers. It is the simplest shared parenting schedule. However, the drawback of this schedule is that parents don't see the children for an entire week. To make this work, many parents take the basic alternating week schedule and add some variations to it. A common variation is to add an evening visit during the week with the other parent.

INSIDER TIP
Custody X Change
(www.custodyxchange.com)
is software that allows you to
create parenting plans.

Other Aspects of a Parenting Plan

MEDICAL COSTS AND HEALTH-CARE INSURANCE

Your plan should explain who will pay for medical and dental costs and who will provide medical insurance for the children.

Your plan can also include information about how the parents will choose health providers for the children, who is responsible for making health appointments, and who will take care of a sick child who needs to stay home.

SCHOOL EXPENSES, EDUCATION, AND EXTRACURRICULAR ACTIVITIES

The education information in your plan includes where your children will attend school, how the parents will choose the children's schools, who pays for school expenses, and who attends parent-teacher conferences and school open houses.

You can also specify how the parents will decide on extracurricular activities for the children, who attends the activities, and who pays for them.

EXCHANGES, OR HANDING OFF CHILDREN BETWEEN THE PARENTS

Specifying details about exchanges (handing off the kids with your ex) helps your schedule run smoothly. You need to decide where exchanges take place, when, and who drives the children for exchanges.

Your plan can also explain how the parents will communicate about schedule changes and rescheduling parenting time. Our Family Wizard (OFW, www.ourfamilywizard.com) is an excellent tool for documenting how exchanges are to take place and reduces the need to communicate directly with your ex about this. To streamline communication, many judges order divorcing parents to use OFW exclusively for scheduling parenting time, the kids' extracurricular activities, and school events. Thus, it makes sense to implement it now, since you may be ordered to utilize it in the future.

PARENTING GUIDELINES FOR RAISING THE CHILDREN

Parenting guidelines are rules in the parenting plan that both parents agree to follow as they raise the children. You can have guidelines about discipline, food and diet, bedtime routines, tobacco and alcohol use around the children, and so on. You can also have rules about who is able to live in the household when a parent has the children.

GUIDELINES FOR THE CHILD-PARENT RELATIONSHIP

Your plan can protect your children's relationships with both parents. You can include guidelines about communication between the children and the parents, such as allowing telephone calls, video calls, and so on.

You can also specify that each parent will encourage the children to have a good relationship with the other parent, that neither parent will speak negatively about the other parent in front of the children, and that the parents will not use children as messengers.

CHILD CARE AND THE RIGHT OF FIRST REFUSAL

Your plan can explain where your child goes for child care when the parents work, how the parents will decide on child care for the child, and who will pay for child care.

You can also include the right of first refusal, which says that if a parent isn't available for scheduled parenting time, the other parent is offered the time first. If this isn't spelled out in the parenting plan, then the unavailable custodial parent is responsible to find alternative child care for the child (like a babysitter or grandparent), but that time does not automatically revert to the other parent.

COMMUNICATION BETWEEN THE PARENTS

Your plan should address parent communication, or how the parents will communicate with each other and what issues they will communicate about. You should also describe how the parents will resolve disputes and make changes to the plan.

Your plan should require that the parents provide updated contact information for each other.

VACATIONS, TRAVEL, AND RELOCATING WITH CHILDREN

Your plan can say how much vacation time each parent has with the children each year and include provisions about traveling and relocating with the children. Travel provisions could include requirements about obtaining and using a passport for the children, providing an itinerary to the other parent when traveling with the children, and/or having a parent give notification when traveling with the children.

Relocating provisions can include that a parent cannot move the children out of a city or county and that notice must be given if a parent is moving the children.

PLANS FOR REVISING THE PLAN

Your plan must contain information about how you and the other parent will revise the plan when one parent needs to make a change. You can create a process for reviewing the plan and making revisions, specify how a parent can suggest changes to the plan, and have a way for the parents to resolve disagreements about revisions to the plan.

Of course, once you negotiate a parenting plan, you should stick to it as best you can, but occasionally a parent will need to adjust the plan, or something will come up that the plan doesn't address. How will you handle these moments? Using an online scheduling program like Our Family Wizard (see above) makes it easy for everyone to stay informed while minimizing direct interactions, but any changes must also be approved by the other party before they take effect. This creates opportunities to negotiate. For instance, you might trade parenting time, such as asking for time to take a vacation with the kids if your ex gets them when he wants, and so on.

CHILDREN WITH SPECIAL NEEDS

You can include provisions in your plan to address any special considerations for your children, or for a specific child, or for your family situation.

CHILD SUPPORT, TAXES, AND FINANCIAL INFORMATION

Your plan can include your child support information, describe how parents will handle reimbursement when one parent pays for something that both parents are responsible for, and specify which parent will claim the child as a dependent for taxes. Typically, parents alternate years in which they claim the child as a dependent, regardless of the time-share arrangement.

OTHER CONSIDERATIONS FOR CREATING A PARENTING PLAN

- Your plan must comply with your state custody guidelines and laws in order for the court to accept it.
- Your child's age impacts what is appropriate for your plan.
- You can include provisions in your plan if one or both parents is in the military.
- When parents live in different states, one state will have jurisdiction over your plan, and you must follow the laws of that state.
- You can include provisions for long-distance travel in your plan if the parents live a long distance from each other.
- You can make a temporary parenting plan when you first separate until you have a permanent custody plan.
- You can modify your plan as your children get older and their needs change.

- If you have multiple children, you can have a split custody arrangement where each parent has custody of different children.

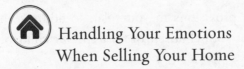

Handling Your Emotions
When Selling Your Home

If you've decided to sell your family home, the most typical scenario is that this is done when the couple divorces, unless there's a practical reason to defer the sale for an extended period after the divorce has been finalized (such as market conditions or until children graduate high school). Once the decision to sell is made, take steps to sell your home without delay. This can be extremely emotional, particularly for women, who can be tied to the family home, even when it makes financial sense to let it go.

Martha's story is demonstrative. Martha and her family had lived in the same house for years. When she and Joe decided to divorce, it was clear that they would have to sell the house in order to fairly divide up their assets. In January, Martha and Joe agreed to move forward with selling the house. Martha dragged her feet, however, in an effort to prolong her time in the family home. In October, Joe took a leave of absence from work to enter a rehab facility for substance abuse. His lawyer filed a motion to reduce the spousal and child support Martha was receiving. Because Martha had delayed listing the house for sale, which would have released liquidity for her, she found herself in a desperate financial situation when Joe reduced his income available for support. She was forced to sell the house during the holidays to raise funds fast, and she got much less than she would have if she had listed the house during the popular summer months when most families are looking for new homes. She also had to uproot her children and enroll them in new schools in the middle of the school year. Don't be Martha.

Here are several pointers for selling your home during a divorce and for keeping emotions from getting in the way.

PICK AN AGENT WHO EMPATHIZES

It can be soothing to work with someone who is compassionate and understands what you are going through. Look for an agent who has experience selling homes during divorce.

Generally, you can tell whether an agent is empathetic when they make their first listing presentation. Ask yourself whether the agent seems to listen and care.

TIME THE SALE WHEN MOST PEOPLE ARE LOOKING

Divorces have their own timetable, but if you can, list the house for sale when the market is busiest to generate multiple offers. If you live in a family-friendly neighborhood and can afford to wait to sell your house, list the house at the beginning of the summer months, when families with school-age children typically move.

SHARE THE COST OF ANY HOME IMPROVEMENTS

If there are improvements that need to be made before listing the house for sale, make them. But coordinate the timing of those improvements so the house is ready at the best time to sell, and have your lawyer negotiate so that your husband pays for them or contributes to them.

DON'T DEMAND THAT PEOPLE PAY FOR YOUR MEMORIES

Unconsciously, some home sellers expect the buyer to pay a premium for the good times they've spent in the property. Without thinking, they add a surcharge for their parties and laughter, for those milestone moments when their kids posed for pictures.

In other words, they set a high price, more than is justified by the state of the property and the current market. But insisting on a steep price, for whatever reason, is an irrational act. An overpriced house won't draw offers during the peak period of its market appeal, usually the first four weeks.

DON'T KEEP THE HOUSE BY RENTING IT

Some women with the means will move after a divorce but decide to retain the family home by converting it to a rental unit. Most of the time, this is an emotional, not a financial, decision, one that merely postpones the moment when they finally let go. Yes, renting buys healing time, but only do so if it's also a prudent financial choice. If you are considering converting your home into a rental unit, first see an accountant or financial planner to be sure it makes sense from a tax and rental-income perspective.

BEFORE THE SALE, PACK UP YOUR MEMORIES

Do you love the deep-rose paint you selected for your living room? Well, painting those walls in oyster white will not only hasten the sale of your property — because neutral tones appeal to more buyers — but it will also help you depersonalize the place. Before you paint, take down the family photos and memorabilia that decorate your walls and pack them away. That will make it easier for potential buyers to picture their own personal items displayed on the walls, and it will make it easier for you to imagine your memories elsewhere.

REMEMBER, MEMORIES ARE ABOUT PEOPLE, NOT PLACES

Every time you look at your yellow guest bedroom, do you think of Grandma, who stayed there each year? Places can seem to hold our memories, but in truth, our memories come with us. What is important about your fondest memories in your house, the place or the people in it? The answer is obvious. To help sever ties, some sellers find comfort in creating a photo album of memories related to the house, including, for example, pictures of Grandma staying in "her" yellow room. Still others benefit from one last ritualistic visit to see the home and neighbors before the final papers are signed.

PUT YOURSELF IN THE BUYERS' LOAFERS

Remember when you first entered the home you now occupy? No doubt you came in without any emotional baggage, thinking solely about the home's appeal and whether it would meet your needs. Seeing the home from the vantage of prospective buyers will help you cut your emotional ties, recognizing it once again as the inanimate object it truly is.

FIND A NEW PLACE YOU CAN GET EXCITED ABOUT

During your home sale, if you find yourself frequently looking back, remind yourself to look forward — to the new place you are moving into. Even if it's smaller, it's your own! Get excited about decorating just the way you want, without having to worry about pleasing a man. Leaving behind a house that undoubtedly contains bad memories from the dark days of your marriage is healthy and something to be excited about. You are going to make a new home with positive, uplifting energy.

 Cultivate the Healing Power of Gratitude

There is a solution to all the overwhelming emotional pain you may be feeling during divorce. The answer may surprise you: It is the attitude of gratitude. Gratitude will get you through the darkest days and pull you out of grief to a new and better life.

You might be thinking, *I feel so devastated. I can't imagine feeling peace ever again!* Or: *Good riddance! I'm so glad to be done with that nightmare husband!* These statements reflect resentment and anger; you feel hurt and are grieving.

WISE WOMEN KNOW
"Gratitude unlocks the fullness of life. It turns what we have into enough, and more. It turns denial into acceptance, chaos to order, confusion to clarity. It can turn a meal into a feast, a house into a home, a stranger into a friend."
— Melody Beattie

As I discuss in chapter 4, grieving during divorce is normal and must be experienced for optimal mental health. You must also, however, put aside or look beyond grief and intentionally focus on positive things for which you are grateful. Gratitude is an immensely powerful force that we can use to expand our happiness, create loving relationships, and even improve our health.

Many scientific studies have found that people who consciously focus on gratitude experience greater emotional well-being and physical health than those who don't (in comparison to control groups). Here is what these studies have found about people who cultivate a grateful outlook:

- They feel better about their lives as a whole.
- They experience greater levels of joy and happiness.
- They feel optimistic about the future.
- They get sick less often.
- They exercise more regularly.
- They have more energy, enthusiasm, determination, and focus.
- They make greater progress toward achieving important personal goals.
- They sleep better and awake feeling refreshed.
- They feel stronger during trying times.
- They enjoy closer family ties.
- They are more likely to help others and offer emotional support.
- They experience fewer symptoms of stress.

If you want more happiness, joy, and energy, gratitude is a crucial quality to cultivate. It is a fullness of heart that moves us from limitation and fear to expansion and love. When we're appreciating something, our ego moves out of the way and we connect with our soul. Gratitude brings our attention into the present, so that we operate without the constraints of past conditioning, which can keep us from reaching our potential.

Even though you may not feel it at first, there are many blessings to be grateful for while recovering from divorce, such as:

- freedom from conflict with your former spouse
- freedom to make your own decisions
- being a positive model for your kids that it is not healthy to stay in a toxic marriage
- the opportunity to parent your children the way you want to when they are at your house
- the occasion to learn how supportive friends and family can be
- the ability to decorate however you want

Many times, the grief of divorce is about the loss of the idealized family life you wanted. For lots of reasons, many women long for a "traditional marriage" with a mom, dad, and kids who live "happily ever after." The realization that this dream will not be happening the way you planned can feel devastating. But it can also open up opportunities for finding a new and better life.

I have found, and have observed, that when divorce finally happens, things have typically been bad for a long time. In fact, life becomes calmer, happier, and much more peaceful once the acting-out husband leaves and the woman is able to create the life she wants for herself and her kids. Sure, it isn't easy being a single mom, but it is much, much better than just surviving in a bad marriage.

Believe you can heal from your divorce. Harboring hurt, resentment, and anger for long periods of time only hurts you — not your ex — and it prevents you from embracing the new life you can create. Do yourself a favor and nurture an attitude of gratitude for everything — however small. You deserve to thrive as a newly single person. And pretty soon, you will see these signs that you are ready to move on:

- You've let go of your anger and embraced your new life.
- You've spent time on yourself and you like who you are.
- You've created a solid family, without the problematic or checked-out spouse.

Keep a Gratitude Journal

Since ancient times, philosophers and sages from every spiritual tradition have taught that cultivating gratitude is a key to experiencing deeper levels of happiness, fulfillment, and well-being.

One of the earliest advocates of a daily gratitude practice was Dutch philosopher Rabbi Baruch Spinoza. In the seventeenth century, he suggested that each day for a month, we ask ourselves the following three questions:

- Who or what inspired me today?
- What brought me happiness today?
- What brought me comfort and deep peace today?

Spinoza believed that this practice would help us find more meaning and joy in our lives and would lead to profound inner transformation. I suggest you answer these questions each day in a gratitude journal. Challenge yourself to not repeat items from the previous days — this will make you look more deeply at all the little things that enhance your life and give you joy, such as:

- your health
- your children
- waking in a warm bed
- the ability to have a fresh start through this divorce
- the ability to choose what your future will be
- the empowerment that comes from knowing that you are creating the life you want to lead

You can write in your journal just before bed, when you wake up in the morning, or just before you meditate. The time of day isn't important; what *is* important is that you consistently take a few moments to consciously focus your mind on your blessings. Commit to writing in your journal about what you are grateful for each day for a month. What we put our attention on expands in our life. By offering gratitude for all the goodness we experience, we're inviting the universe to give us more and more of what we want.

Write a Thank-You Letter

Make a list of at least five people who have had a profound impact on your life. Choose one and write a thank-you letter expressing gratitude for all the gifts you've received from that person. If possible, deliver your gratitude letter in person.

In studies of people who have practiced this form of gratitude, the results have been amazing. Often the recipient of the letter had no idea what an impact he or she had had on the other person and were deeply touched by the expression of such authentic gratitude.

While we may often thank people verbally, the written word can be even more powerful because someone has taken the time to write their appreciation. A letter can also be reread and treasured, creating joy and love that will continue to ripple out into the universe.

Take a Gratitude Walk

This is a particularly useful practice when you're feeling down or filled with stress and worry. Set aside twenty minutes (or longer if you can) and walk in your neighborhood, through a park, around your office, or somewhere in nature. As you walk, consider the many things for which you are grateful, such as:

- nurturing relationships
- material comforts

- a body that allows you to experience the world
- a mind that allows you to understand yourself and your essential spiritual nature

Pay attention to your senses — everything you're seeing, hearing, feeling, smelling, and maybe even tasting — and see how many things you can find to feel grateful for. Breathe, pause, and be grateful for the air that is filling your lungs and making your life possible. This is a powerful way to shift your mood and open to the flow of abundance that always surrounds you.

CHAPTER 6

Settlement

"Those who know when to fight and when not to fight are victorious."
— Sun Tzu, *The Art of War*

*T*he vast majority of divorces never go to trial. It's estimated that 95 percent of divorces are settled out of court. In relatively simple cases, a settlement can be worked out without much contention, and often in mediation. Divorces involving complex financial issues or extraordinarily contentious or narcissistic spouses can require many months or even years of detailed work by teams of specialized professionals, including attorneys, forensic accountants, valuation experts, real estate appraisers, vocational consultants, and so on. Then, with each side working for their own client's best interest, they try to negotiate a settlement agreement. How long this takes depends on many factors, including the preparedness of both parties, their willingness to work toward a solution, and the complexity of the issues to be decided. When complete, the settlement agreement is signed by both parties and filed with the court.

If, on the other hand, you do not reach a settlement, buckle your seat belt and open your checkbook. A two-day divorce trial can cost $25,000 in legal fees alone. For this price, you will get to air all your dirty laundry, and it will be permanently recorded in a publicly accessible document. In addition, a complete stranger, the judge, will make determinations about your finances, property, and children that will permanently impact you and your family members. For all the right reasons, it makes sense to work toward settlement and to avoid going to trial.

The right frame of mind is important in order to reach a settlement. It is important to remember that in divorce there are no "winners." The sooner you accept this fact of life, the sooner you will be ready to negotiate a resolution to your conflicts. In most cases, you will be better off negotiating issues on your own, so that they meet your real needs, rather than letting a judge do it. For instance, when it comes to a property split, the judge will chop things roughly in half, and that's that. But what if you want to stay in the house until your youngest child completes high school, and at that point, you'd be happy to sell the house and split the equity with your ex? A judge may not allow that.

The same is true when it comes to your parenting plan. If you ask a judge to order it, they might order a plan that is "fair" on the surface but that pleases no one. Only you and your ex know what your needs are and those of your children. Ideally, through negotiation, you and your ex can create a plan that's flexible enough to accommodate the changes that will naturally occur as your children grow and their schedules require modification. In this way, you can avoid having to go back to court repeatedly to obtain modifications to the parenting plan over time.

What your divorce settlement cannot do is right the moral wrongs between you and your spouse. Regardless of who was "right" and who was "wrong," that is not going to get resolved through your divorce. There is zero benefit to dragging out the process or taking your spouse to court simply because you feel that you were wronged. Treat this like the dissolution of a business partnership, and you will be the "winner."

DIVORCE HACKS

 Negotiate from a Position of Strength

In order to reach a settlement, you will need to compromise. Both sides will need to feel that they are getting what they want, or at least getting what's most important to them. So be prepared to bargain, while still negotiating from a position of strength. Here are several things you can do to increase your leverage and ensure that you get what you want out of a settlement.

Conduct Discovery

Serving your spouse with discovery can be an effective way to leverage a settlement you want. For example, if your husband has his own business, he probably won't want your attorney scrutinizing his taxes. And no one likes to have their deposition taken under oath.

Consider my client Sharon. Her husband, Ron, ran his own business and claimed that he was losing money. As is often the case, the losses coincided with his filing for divorce. In the meantime, Ron was driving a new Mercedes and taking his girlfriend on expensive trips to exotic locations. We served Ron with discovery requests demanding his business records and set his deposition. During his deposition, Ron could not answer questions about the business expenses he had claimed on his taxes. The next day, Ron's counsel sent over a settlement offer that was very favorable for Sharon.

There are several types of formal discovery that can be effectively used to obtain information from your spouse and increase your chances of obtaining what you want during settlement negotiations. You can serve requests for production (formally asking for documents) and interrogatories (written questions), take depositions (interrogating your husband under oath), and subpoena business records (from banks or employers). Your spouse (or the third party) must respond under oath and provide what is requested.

The only drawback is that discovery is expensive, so you will need to weigh the pros and cons with your lawyer. But if your budget permits, serving discovery can be a powerful, effective tool to obtain information and get what you want from a spouse who doesn't want their finances scrutinized or to testify under oath.

Compare Spousal Support Options

In order to negotiate effectively, you need to know whether you or your spouse are eligible for "permanent" or only temporary spousal support, the amount of support, and the duration. "Permanent" spousal support is something of a misnomer. It does not mean that a nonworking spouse from a long-term marriage is entitled to lifetime support. That may have been true during our mothers' era, but it is no longer the case in most states. Permanent spousal support is awarded in only 10 to 15 percent of cases that go to court, and what qualifies as a long-term marriage varies (in California, it's over ten years). Spousal support is meant to bridge the gap between divorce and the time it takes for a spouse to obtain employment or resources that meet their cost-of-living needs. For instance, in California, for marriages of less than ten years, spousal support is presumed to be no longer in duration than half the length of the marriage.

Permanent spousal support is determined by evaluating a lengthy list of considerations, including the standard of living during the marriage, employment, income, earning capacity, whether a spouse took time off from work to raise minor children, and the health of each party. Permanent spousal support orders are typically slightly lower than temporary support orders. The court cannot use a support calculator like DissoMaster in the determination of permanent support. It must analyze all the subjective factors identified above in making an order for permanent support. However, many lawyers and mediators will run the DissoMaster and use it in settlement negotiations to arrive at a ballpark figure for permanent support.

Permanent spousal support terminates when the recipient spouse remarries or either spouse dies. In Massachusetts, alimony terminates when the recipient spouse cohabitates with another person for at least three months. In some states, alimony terminates when the payor spouse reaches retirement age.

If you or your spouse may be entitled to permanent support, you will want to consider whether to propose or accept a lump-sum payment of spousal support versus monthly payments over time. With a lump-sum payment, there is typically an agreement that the court's jurisdiction to award support terminates, which provides the benefit of closure for the paying party. For either party, a lump-sum payment might also be the smart choice financially, but it depends on what you think may happen to you both in the future.

For instance, if payments are made over time and the payor suddenly makes significantly more income, the recipient can seek a modification of support upward. This happened to Cecilia when her ex was promoted from the assistant coach of a professional sports team to the head coach and his salary tripled. Cecilia was able to go to court and substantially increase her spousal support payments. Then again, if you are awarded permanent spousal support and think you might remarry, you might want a lump-sum payout, since support payments stop when you remarry. If you are the payer, and you think your spouse might remarry, insist on monthly payments over time rather than a lump-sum payment, since those payments will stop once your spouse remarries.

Evaluate Tax and Long-Term Consequences

With the help of your financial adviser or forensic accountant, your attorney can evaluate different settlement scenarios to achieve what will serve you best over the long run. You need to consider more than bottom-line dollar amounts. You want to consider the value of any retirement assets, your home and spousal support, and the tax consequences. For example, it may make sense to negotiate for a greater share of the retirement benefits in exchange for less spousal support, since spousal support doesn't last forever and is taxable to the recipient for divorces finalized in 2018. Starting in 2019, however, spousal support will no longer be tax deductible for the payer and taxable to the recipient. Depending on your housing needs, you may negotiate to stay in the house until the children finish school and have your spouse make the mortgage payments in lieu of child support. Or you may decide to waive your share of the family business in exchange for the family home.

> **INSIDER TIP**
> *There may be reimbursable expenses that are negotiable. For example, if you stay in the marital home, your spouse may seek the reasonable rental value of that home from the date of separation. If you pay for the children's expenses with your separate income, you are entitled to reimbursement. If you use your separate property to contribute to the acquisition or improvement of community property, you have a right to reimbursement. Understand what reimbursements apply under your state's laws so that you can negotiate accordingly.*

My client Gail received a settlement offer from her spouse that proposed a spousal support buyout and that the family home would be sold and the proceeds equally divided. Gail's husband, John, would keep his retirement assets and the family business. Gail hadn't worked in thirty years. Initially, Gail thought that this was a good offer. However, after her financial adviser calculated the tax consequences of the proposed settlement, it became clear that Gail would run out of money before she turned sixty-five. Of course, this was unacceptable. We served John with written discovery and set his deposition. With discovery deadlines looming and John about to be deposed under oath, he offered Gail the family home and 60 percent of his retirement benefits — a significant improvement over the initial offer she received.

Deciding to Negotiate Directly with Your Ex

Divorce attorneys often advise their clients not to talk to their spouse. Why? Because they don't want the case to settle. Lawyers benefit when a case drags on because they can keep billing. But often you can settle by dealing with your spouse directly — the key is timing.

For instance, consider my client Mary, whose story I introduce in chapter 2 (page 37). Her husband, Mark, walked out on her after over thirty years, not long after he claimed to have been fired from his high-paying job. Mary was blindsided when Marked filed for divorce, and very early in the proceedings, Mark's lawyer sent over a settlement offer proposing that Mary waive spousal support, since Mark was fired from his job. In exchange, Mary would receive half of Mark's retirement assets, and the family home would be sold and the proceeds split in half. Mary thought this offer seemed fair, since Mark was unemployed.

However, after some undercover sleuthing, Mary learned the truth: Mark had not been fired; he had taken an early retirement, and he was having an affair with one of his coworkers. Mary also discovered that the day after Mark walked out, he received a million-dollar distribution from his employer. When asked about this, Mark's attorney claimed Mary was not entitled to any of this distribution because Mark received it after they separated.

Armed with this knowledge, we served Mark with written discovery and set his and his boss's depositions. We also filed a motion asking the court to order Mark to undergo a vocational examination to determine his earning capacity, since he had voluntarily left his job.

With Mark's deposition looming and a court date approaching, Mary asked me whether she should reach out to Mark to try

> **INSIDER TIP**
> *You can often achieve a favorable settlement by negotiating directly with your spouse while litigation is pending. Timing is key and should be discussed with your attorney.*

to resolve things. We knew that Mark did not want to be deposed or sit for a vocational examination. While the pressure was on, Mary began communicating with Mark via email. On Christmas Eve, just days before his deposition, Mark agreed to give Mary half of the million-dollar distribution he received from his employer, half of his retirement benefits, and the family home. Mary obtained what she needed by negotiating with Mark at the right moment, when she had the most leverage.

 Mediation — How to Get What You Want

Mediation is a negotiation that is facilitated by a neutral mediator. Sometimes divorcing couples work only with a mediator, who helps them split their assets and liabilities, deal with future support, make parenting plans, and so on. This works well if your divorce is simple and less contentious. If your case is complex, or full of conflict, and you have hired an attorney, you can still resolve your case through mediation without going to trial.

When John and Elizabeth began mediation, they both immediately demanded "school-night" custody of their seven-year-old daughter, Ashley. It became such a stalemate that it appeared inevitable that they were headed to trial. As a last resort, the mediator took each spouse aside and asked them privately to explain the goal of their custody demands — what did John and Elizabeth really want?

What the mediator found was that John and Elizabeth both viewed having their daughter during the week — instead of weekends only — as the way to have the most influence over her life and to have the most quality time with her. The mediator asked each parent to create a schedule of the time they could reasonably spend with Ashley during the week, blocking out their work schedules and the time Ashley was in school.

John's schedule required him to work until 7 PM two nights a week, with Fridays and his weekends off. Elizabeth's schedule was much looser during the week, though she often got called into work on Friday night. The mediator pointed out to John how little time he would actually spend with Ashley if he got his demand, which he was overlooking in his quest to win this battle. To Elizabeth, the mediator stressed that it might not be practical for her to have Ashley on every weeknight, since many Friday nights she would need to call a sitter.

Because Elizabeth and John lived in the same town, the solution became very clear and simple: Elizabeth would have Ashley from Monday afternoon through Friday morning. At the end of the school day on Friday, Ashley would get off the bus at John's house and stay with him until Monday morning, when she got on the bus to go to school. John also negotiated more parenting time during school vacations. As a means of making sure John still retained shared control over Ashley's school-week activities, Elizabeth agreed to send duplicates of any permission slips and school paperwork to John on a weekly basis. In the end, what happened? Both John and Elizabeth were able to get what they really wanted — quality time and influence. Would a judge have taken the time to get to the heart of this matter in the same way the mediator did? Maybe, but maybe not. Just as importantly, mediation helped resolve this issue without going to court.

What should you do if you are headed to mediation, or if you'd like to explore this option? Here are some steps to ensure mediation is successful and results in the divorce settlement you want.

Educate Yourself or Hire Advisers

In mediation, you retain the services of a professional mediator. The mediator is neutral; unlike a lawyer, they cannot give you legal or financial advice. The mediator's job is to help you and your spouse negotiate any issues, such as division of property, allocation of debts, support, parenting plans, and the like. It's up to you to be thoroughly knowledgeable about your financial affairs, what assets you own, what the assets are worth, your debts and obligations, the nature and value of any retirement plans or accounts, how much you will need to live on after the divorce, what the needs of the children are, and so forth. If you are uncertain or unclear about any of these issues, you need to educate yourself or hire someone to help.

> WISE WOMEN KNOW
> *Successful negotiation*
> *requires planning, strategy,*
> *and discipline.*

For instance, do you feel comfortable making a game plan for your future? Do you know what you want to be doing in five or ten years? Do you feel confident negotiating your divorce settlement so that the future unfolds the way you want it to? As I say, even in mediation, hiring an attorney is prudent, but depending on the complexity of your case, you may want to retain an accountant and some of the other professionals I've discussed.

Of course, your attorney will give you legal advice and represent you in mediation. Most mediators will ask for a mediation brief a week in advance of the mediation. Your attorney will work with you to put together a mediation brief that outlines how you wish to divide up your assets and debts, what you want for spousal support, and if you have children, a proposed custody and parenting plan.

Get Control of Your Emotions

In most states, the law sets forth how marital affairs must generally be arranged. A good lawyer not only will explain how the law works, they can predict with high accuracy what a judge might do in your case. If that's so, why do some couples find it so hard to settle? The problem is often their emotions. Feelings of hatred, rage, betrayal, abandonment, grief, and sadness are normal, but they interfere with negotiations. To help manage your emotions, get counseling, especially while you're trying to reach a divorce settlement.

You cannot make good decisions about your future if you are highly emotional. Anger in a divorce negotiation will hurt you, not help you. When you become angry, you lose the ability to think clearly. Your prefrontal cortex literally shuts down. Worse, it will not come back to full functioning for hours. Your spouse may deliberately trigger you, insult you, disrespect you, or ignore you during the negotiation. Keep your cool. Let your spouse become angry and upset and watch how their ability to make good decisions goes out the window. You can use emotions to your advantage as long as they are not your emotions.

Choose a Good Mediator

Anyone can be a mediator. There are no licenses for becoming a mediator in most states. However, choose a professional mediator who has gone to school and taken graduate courses in conflict resolution. Don't choose a mediator who has taken a basic forty-hour mediation course, unless that mediator has been practicing full-time for at least seven years. Experience counts.

Know What You Really Want

Negotiating a divorce settlement is not unlike buying a used car. You need to know what is important to you (reliable transportation) and not be distracted or misled by what isn't (paint color, leather seats); you risk buyer's remorse otherwise. With every issue in your divorce settlement, ask yourself that all-important question: What do I really want? If you say you want the house, is it really the house? Or is it staying in the same community, owning rather than renting, or wanting your kids to have a sense of stability? Maybe you will get the house, but maybe you can get what you really want — or even something better — without it (perhaps by using the house as a negotiating point). Keep what you really want firmly in mind as you enter negotiations, and then be open to other possibilities or ways to achieve it.

Consider the Other Side, and Don't Assume

We all have certain expectations in terms of what is possible during a negotiation, but these assumptions can sometimes hold us back. A common mistake is to analyze a negotiation only from our own perspective. When diplomats discuss the terms of a cease-fire, for example, they always have to think of the other side: Is this a deal that the other side will entertain? What do they really want, and how can I give it to them and still get what I want?

Mary was able to get Mark to agree to give her what she wanted (the family house and half of his retirement assets) because she understood what he wanted — and didn't want. He didn't want to be deposed during the holidays or sit for a vocational examination. He wanted to be done with the divorce so he could travel with his girlfriend. Mary used what he really wanted to her advantage in negotiations.

> INSIDER TIP
> *Broaden your perspective about what is negotiable by considering the situation from your spouse's perspective. What does he want out of this?*

Most women approach mediation by focusing only on getting what they want. They don't consider how to use their spouse's desires as a bargaining tool. Don't think of a negotiation as a zero-sum game. Think of it as solving a joint problem — how can you and your spouse both get what you really want?

List Your Goals and Your Bargaining Chips

As you prepare for mediation, make a two-column list. In one, list all your demands, the things you want: the house, the flat-screen TV, your stock portfolio, your desired child custody arrangement, and so on. In the other column, list your bargaining chips. What will you give in exchange for the items in the first list? Ideally, name relevant or related items for each goal. If you get the flat-screen TV, will you give up the laptop or pay $800 cash? If you get the stock portfolio, will you give up a larger percent of your company 401K, and so on. Show the list to your attorney first, so he or she can see from the outset how much you are willing to compromise. Your attorney can offer suggestions and feedback on your list.

Be Patient

It would be nice if your spouse could be equally reflective upon entering mediation, but don't expect this to be the case. If there is a standoff on certain issues, this is where the mediator comes in to help. Your ex will think he's won a victory (let him, it's good for further negotiations!), but you will know that you just got exactly what you wanted. Sometimes it can take several rounds of mediation to settle a case. Understand, this is part of the process. When you experience frustration and impatience, you are most likely anxious, and you will want to rush to the conclusion to rid yourself of this anxiety. That would be a mistake. If you can out-patience your spouse, you can sometimes get a better deal than if you rushed through the process.

> **WISE WOMEN KNOW**
> *Patience is a virtue for a good negotiator. Breathe, pause, relax. Use your mindful meditation practice to support you and to maintain your composure.*

Ask for a Draft Settlement Agreement

Discuss with your attorney in advance of mediation your desire to obtain a written settlement agreement before you leave the mediation. The agreement will be a draft of what will ultimately become a stipulated judgment, the court order that becomes the divorce decree. The document should include division of major assets and debts, spousal support, child support, and the parenting plan if there are minor children. The goal is to have both parties sign a draft settlement agreement before they leave mediation.

However, do not feel pressured to sign a settlement agreement if you have doubts. You can always walk away from the mediation, take time to consider the proposal, and continue to negotiate. I have participated in mediations that have gone long into the night, and the client feels exhausted and pressured to reach an agreement. In those instances, it may be better to step away, clear your head, and return to negotiations at a later time.

If you do reach an acceptable agreement during mediation, have *your* lawyer draft the settlement agreement. This will give you greater control over what it does and does not include. Whoever drafts the document during the mediation will typically be the drafter of the stipulated judgment. This can be a lengthy and expensive undertaking, but if you have the resources, it's worth it to maintain control.

How a Forensic Accountant Can Help

Financial issues are among the most contentious in divorce proceedings. Forensic accountants (most often CPAs) possess unique skills that allow them to provide valuable support to divorcing spouses and their attorneys. Employing the expertise of a qualified forensic accountant can make a considerable difference in the outcome of your divorce and your future. A forensic accountant has the tools and knowledge to do the following:

- Value businesses and professional practices for clients such as doctors, lawyers, accountants, and other professionals
- Separate business expenses versus personal expenses to ensure the business is valued accurately
- Trace property to determine what is community and separate property
- Determine monthly cash flow available for child and spousal support
- Consider tax ramifications of various settlement scenarios

- Work with attorneys and a mediator to develop an equitable settlement

When to Hire a Forensic Accountant

It is typical for one spouse to assume the money management role during the life of a marriage, and seldom do both spouses have equal knowledge of the couple's financial affairs. Consequently, in a divorce proceeding, the money-manager spouse holds an unfair advantage, and this is frequently utilized to achieve a more favorable settlement. In some cases, capitalizing on this advantage may escalate to the level of fraud by the money-manager spouse. The higher-earning spouse has strong financial incentives to understate income in order to reduce alimony or child support payments. Additionally, one or both of the spouses may attempt to hide assets they wish to retain postdivorce.

Through an examination of financial records, a forensic accountant plays a vital role in uncovering hidden or transferred assets and income that directly impact both support and equitable distribution. Forensic accountants are uniquely qualified for this role because of their knowledge and experience in financial document analysis, accounting principles, and auditing techniques.

A forensic investigation is advisable and should be considered in situations where one spouse is suspected of concealing income or assets or when it is the only means for procuring financial information. It may also be beneficial when there is a closely held business or a highly compensated spouse. And a forensic accountant's services can be invaluable when assessing the tax ramifications of a proposed settlement.

For example, Mary received a settlement proposal from her high-earning spouse that looked good on paper. However, after her forensic accountant analyzed the proposed cash flow available for support over her anticipated lifetime and took into account taxes and inflation, it became clear that Mary would run out of money before she turned seventy. Obviously, this was unacceptable, since her husband had the ability and opportunity to provide adequate support to maintain their marital standard of living in the form of marital assets. With the help of the forensic accountant, Mary negotiated a settlement that included assets sufficient to provide income and security for the duration of Mary's anticipated lifetime.

Uncovering Hidden Income and Assets

If the road leading to divorce is long and rocky, the spouse with the higher income may attempt to hide, transfer, or defer income or assets in anticipation of a divorce settlement. The spouse may accomplish this by withdrawing unreported cash from a closely held business, manipulating receipts and expenses of a closely held business, transferring cash to other individuals or entities, or deferring the receipt of a bonus or other compensation until after the divorce is settled.

Detecting hidden, transferred, or deferred income is complicated and difficult, but forensic accountants have several effective techniques for uncovering it. These techniques include the analysis of the family's lifestyle to determine whether the level of reported income is sufficient to support the family's expenditures, an examination of the couple's net worth at two or more points in time to determine whether the reported income during the period is consistent with the change in net worth, and an analysis of bank deposits.

The methods also include the analysis of individual, fiduciary, and business tax returns, the examination of personal and business financial statements or loan applications, and public records searches. Detailed forensic review of disbursements made from bank and brokerage accounts can prove valuable in identifying situations where one spouse has attempted to dissipate marital assets in anticipation of the separation. In many situations, identifying unreported income is a very effective tool in negotiating a favorable settlement.

Investigating Closely Held Businesses

A closely held business is often a prime vehicle for hiding assets or income. A forensic examination of the business can be worthwhile, especially when the opposing spouse is actively involved in the day-to-day operations and is suspected of using business assets or income for his personal benefit in excess of reported income. Often, the owner of a closely held business will take advantage of his control over the company's finances in order to extract additional compensation by either the payment of personal obligations using corporate funds, engaging in non–arm's length transactions with related entities, or through the payment of excessive perquisites (such as homes, cars, and so on).

When examining a closely held business, a forensic accountant will determine whether hidden income or assets exist, whether business funds have been used to purchase personal assets and pay personal expenses, whether the owner-spouse has been intentionally reducing the profitability of the business, and whether there have been inappropriate related-party transactions. The examination will include a detailed review of business records and practices, including internal controls, as well as issues unique to the wider industry. The investigation typically yields a financial road map to the hidden value of the business.

The business appraiser typically prepares a valuation for the entity based upon the "normalized" income for the business. That is, the appraiser's valuation is based upon the earnings that a third-party purchaser could theoretically expect to receive upon acquiring the business. Since a closely held business is often the largest asset subject to equitable distribution in a marital dissolution, obtaining an accurate business valuation is essential.

Get to Work — How Your Job Affects a Settlement

Sharon arrived in my office with hunched shoulders and downcast eyes. She explained that her marriage of twenty-five years was over and that she was going to start looking for a job as a secretary. Sharon was fifty-five years old and had never worked as a secretary. She was depressed.

Sharon is now the successful CEO of a multimillion-dollar company. How did this happen? Through strategic divorce negotiations.

Before Sharon married, her passion was fashion and travel. When she married Bill, she turned that passion into a successful clothing company that focused on high-end European designs. When Sharon began having children, she shifted her focus to the company's domestic operations, and Bill traveled and handled the overseas suppliers. After the arrival of their third child, Sharon stepped away from the business to raise the kids. The company thrived as long as the marriage was working. But when the marriage went sideways, so did the company. The company lost its biggest supplier, and revenues plummeted. When Sharon arrived in my office, the company was on the verge of declaring bankruptcy, and she thought her only recourse was to try to find a secretarial job. Of course, trying to find a job at the age of fifty-five is not easy.

I envisioned a different outcome for Sharon. This company was her baby. It was her idea and her passion. What if we could find a way for her to keep the company, and she could reinvent herself? At first, Sharon was reluctant. She had three kids — now teenagers — and she couldn't wrap her head around the idea of being a single mom and running a struggling company. But I encouraged her to envision a new and better life, one where she was the boss and her company was thriving.

Together we drafted a settlement proposal whereby Sharon would take over the company; in exchange, Bill would receive the building the company occupied. It took several four-way settlement conferences — meetings between Sharon, Bill, and the attorneys — but eventually we hammered out a deal.

Today, Sharon is the CEO of a thriving fashion company, she travels the world in connection with her work, and she is raising three wonderful teenagers. Sure, she was challenged at times to juggle the kids while getting the company back on track, but she did it. And Sharon is literally transformed. She emanates positive energy and enthusiasm. She is her own woman.

As Sharon's story demonstrates, timing is everything. But what about the opposite scenario? What can you do if you are the primary breadwinner, and you don't want to write a hefty spousal support check to your ex each month?

The Breadwinner Wife and Spousal Support

In today's world, wives are frequently the family breadwinner, which means that during divorce, their husbands are the ones asking for spousal support. The bigger the difference in earnings and the longer you were married, the larger the support payment will be. What can a woman do to minimize this obligation?

The general standard, which applies equally to both spouses, is that maintenance can be awarded if one spouse lacks sufficient property, including marital property, to provide for their reasonable needs and expenses and is unable to support themselves through appropriate employment.

Clients often ask whether they should delay working or quit their jobs to reduce their income during a divorce, to minimize their obligation to provide maintenance to their spouse. Strategy is important here. If you do not work or are underemployed, and if you are healthy and able, the judge will likely order you to undergo a vocational examination to determine how much money you are capable of earning. That phantom income will be imputed to you in making the support calculation. So, choosing not to work, or intentionally earning less, can backfire.

Kelly's work strategy paid long-term dividends. At one time, Kelly had worked in finance at a large accounting firm and had earned more than her husband, Brad, but she had left her job to raise the children. When problems arose in her marriage, she decided to file for divorce. She knew, however, that if she didn't have a job, the court could impute the income that she was capable of earning in her previous job when making its support determination. Kelly took on some contract work for a local accountant, which provided some income and also flexibility so that she could be available for her children after school. When Brad asked the court to conduct a vocational examination with the intention of using her prior six-figure income in the support calculation, the judge refused because Kelly had a job and was also taking care of the kids. This strategy worked because Kelly received more support than she would have received if she hadn't gone back to work. Once the divorce was finalized, Kelly increased her work hours and income and was on her way to financial freedom and independence.

To reduce your exposure to alimony, consider the following actions:

Action steps for the breadwinner wife

- **Reduce current household expenses:** The monthly household expenses are used to determine "need," which in turn is used to determine support. Reducing the household expenses reduces the benchmark "need" utilized in the support calculation.
- **Establish a precedent of the husband supporting his own needs with little or no financial support from you:** If your husband can meet his own needs, then he doesn't have an argument that he needs support from you.
- **Help get the husband a job or more education:** Whatever

you can do to help your husband become self-sufficient will strengthen your argument that he does not need support from you.

- **Maximize time with the children:** This is the right thing and the smart thing to do. Child support is determined by running a computer program, such as the Disso-Master, which utilizes the time children spend with each party. The more time they spend with you, the less you will owe in child support.

- **Allow a temporary disability to improve:** One of the factors in the support determination is the relative health of the parties. If your husband suffers from a temporary disability, allow him to regain his health before filing so that he is able to work and contribute to his support.

- **Reduce income available for support:** If income is trending down, it would make sense to hold off the divorce to use a lower income in calculating maintenance. If you are self-employed, confer with your accountant and determine whether you can minimize your income available for support by claiming additional business expenses or other deductions.

- **Request the husband undergo a vocational evaluation:** If your husband is shirking his obligation to work or is under-earning, request he agree to submit to a vocational evaluation for purposes of imputing income in the support determination. Sometimes just the suggestion that you will go down this path will improve your position during settlement negotiations.

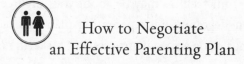

How to Negotiate an Effective Parenting Plan

Negotiating a parenting plan can be challenging. Moms tend to believe that they have innate rights because they are the mother, and dads also want to maintain a relationship with the children. How do you resolve this imbalance? The way in which you negotiate your parenting plan can impact how decisions are made. In chapter 5 (page 144), I discuss what a parenting plan should include, and this section offers three helpful tips for getting what you want during negotiations.

Check Your Facts and Come Prepared

Negotiating a parenting plan is an unfamiliar process to most. First, learn as much as you can about the child custody laws in your state, since these have a direct impact on your plan. For example, Jane was insistent that she have full custody of the children and that Robert have limited visitation. Jane believed that a mother had an innate right to be declared the "resident" parent, despite the fact that the law in her state did not give mothers that inherent right. Jane was the breadwinner and frequently traveled in connection with her work. Robert was the stay-at-home parent with primary responsibility for the children. Jane's plan had zero chance with a judge given the laws in her state. Jane burned through a lot of attorney hours, money, and angst before coming to terms with this reality.

Next, think about the outcome you want for your family. Consider your children's needs and how you can best serve them when negotiating your parenting plan. When a judge rules on a parenting plan, the legal standard is the "children's best interest." This is not the time to work out your power struggles with your spouse. Put the kids' interests first and the rest will fit into place.

Be Open, Calm, and Polite

No matter what your feelings may be about your divorce, it is important that you negotiate your parenting plan as peacefully as possible. It might not be a speedy process, but bickering or not co-operating won't help move it along any faster. Stay calm and remain polite throughout negotiations. Allowing your emotions to get the best of you could lead to dead ends and stalemates, making the process even longer and more complicated than it could have been. Stay focused on getting this done for your kids.

Negotiating a parenting plan requires much discussion. As such, recognize that you both have things to say, and you both are allowed to speak. Take turns speaking and listening. When speaking, be as articulate and straightforward as possible about what you want from the plan, without becoming accusatory or offensive. Talk to your spouse the way you would speak to a business associate. When it's your turn to listen, give your spouse your full attention. Don't interrupt or reply in haste. Consider what he has to say, then respond.

A settlement requires compromise; the plan you agree to will probably not be exactly what you want. The same will probably be true for your spouse. Be open to new ideas and approaches during negotiations. Think first about what will serve your children's well-being. If something does, consider going with it or negotiating the proposal so that it is closer to what you originally wanted. A little flexibility can go a long way in helping you reach agreements that work for your whole family.

Consider Using a Therapist to Negotiate

Attorneys are expensive and not always best suited to work through the nuances of your parenting plan. If your children have been working with a therapist, and you are having difficulty communicating with your spouse, consider having the therapist assist you in negotiating a parenting plan. It may be more effective and will be less expensive than using your attorney.

Stacey and Kevin were deadlocked over their parenting plan, and we were headed to trial. Two of their three children were moving back and forth between their separate households quite well, but Ellen, the twelve-year-old daughter, refused to go to Kevin's house. Kevin was so locked into a power struggle over Ellen that he called the police repeatedly when she refused to go to his house. This only made matters worse. Ellen began to cut class and her grades were dropping.

I suggested that Stacey, Kevin, and Ellen meet with Ellen's therapist to break the deadlock. In that safe place, Ellen was able to express her feelings — that she just needed to feel safe, and for now at least, that meant being at Mom's house. When Kevin heard this directly from Ellen, rather than his soon-to-be-ex-wife, he agreed. And after a couple of months at her mom's house, Ellen began to visit her dad and spend time with him regularly.

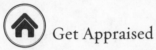 Get Appraised

You can expect discussions about your home's worth to be a key aspect of negotiating a settlement, since it is usually one of the main marital assets. This means you will probably need to obtain a professional real estate appraisal before you can settle. Why is this so important? Because if, for example, you wish to stay in the family home, you will need sufficient other assets to "buy out" your husband in order to "equalize" him. Say the house is appraised at a million dollars; to keep the house yourself, you will have to give your spouse $500,000 worth of stock, retirement funds, other real estate, or cash to buy him out. Thus, the valuation of the family home is often a hotly contested issue, and sometimes each spouse will obtain their own appraisal and present it during negotiations. How does the appraisal process work, and what happens if you end up with two differing appraisals?

Often, your attorney will be able to recommend a reputable appraisal firm that will give an unbiased, arm's-length, and standalone valuation of your property. Your attorney can arrange for the appraisal report on your behalf, or they can leave the choice of appraiser up to you and your spouse. If possible, the best scenario may be for you and your spouse to agree to hire one appraiser.

The fee for the appraisal is paid for by the divorcing parties — typically split down the middle, unless each spouse orders a separate appraisal. Appraisers collect their fees in differing ways. Sometimes, it's billed to the attorney that retains them on your behalf. Other times, it's collected from the spouse that stays in the home during the property visit.

The appraisal process begins with a "property visit." The appraiser examines the house and asks questions of the homeowner, who should be present, such as, "Are there any problems or concerns with the property? Any special circumstances I should know about?" The appraiser will take measurements, look into crawl spaces, check for updates to plumbing and electricity and any other amenities, and do a visual inspection of the siding, roof, and yard. The appraiser is looking for features or conditions that would raise or lower the home's value compared to other similar homes in the neighborhood. Sometimes, features that the homeowner greatly values may not contribute to the home's value in proportion to the price paid for them — such as a swimming pool or wine cellar.

Following the property visit, the appraiser compares your property with at least three similar properties in the surrounding vicinity that have sold within the past six months. The sale prices of the sold homes determine their value. Using a standardized template, the appraiser makes an itemized comparison between your house and each of the "comps." The appraiser compares the number of bedrooms and bathrooms, square footage, existence of a fireplace or view, the general condition, and so forth.

Finally, using their professional expertise and judgment, the appraiser will make a definitive analysis, giving the most weight to the comparable home that most closely resembles yours. Thus, a market-based value is arrived at for your home. Often, this final analysis is explained in narrative form and includes comments and clarifications, as necessary.

Professional appraisers are bound to practice fairness and objectivity through USPAP (Uniform Standards of Professional

Appraisal Practice), and for members of the Appraisal Institute, the Code of Professional Ethics. Confidentiality is a major requirement. An appraiser is not allowed to divulge information to either divorcing party or their attorneys before the final valuation is made.

If each spouse obtains a separate appraisal, you could end up with two different valuations for the marital property. In this case, typically, a mediator splits the difference: The two differing values are added, then divided by two, and that value is used for the purposes of settlement.

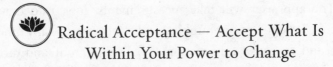

Radical Acceptance — Accept What Is Within Your Power to Change

What is radical acceptance? Let's start with what it is not. It is not approval of whatever happened that led to divorce. It does not mean that you are excusing bad behavior or that you are okay with it. You are not absolving the person who hurt you of all responsibility. You are not allowing any betrayal or infidelity.

You are acknowledging reality so that you do not have to suffer and so that you can choose to change it. Fighting reality only intensifies our emotional reaction and creates suffering. Suffering is optional.

Radical acceptance requires that you look upon yourself, others, and the world in an entirely new way. You must be willing to let go of your ideas about how things "should be" and simply accept the way things *are*…in this present moment. When you radically accept something, you completely release judgment and avoid any attempts to fight against or change what happened. For example, if you were to radically accept this present moment in time, it means that you would acknowledge

> **WISE WOMEN KNOW**
> *Suffering is optional. Through acceptance of the way things are, we free ourselves from the past and create a new and better future.*

that everything that "is" right now is the result of a very long and complicated chain of events. You are responsible for *some* of this present moment, and you are not responsible for *some* of this present moment. Many events have happened to bring you to precisely where you are right now.

Once we accept reality, we can consider if we'd like to change it. We can say: "Okay, this happened. How do I want to handle it?" In other words, practicing acceptance actually leads the way to problem solving. By practicing radical acceptance, you still react. But your reactions are less intense, and they don't last as long as they would if you focused on fighting what is. Another benefit is that you typically spend less time thinking about the situation. Then, when you do think about it, this triggers less emotional pain for you. People often describe a feeling of being "lighter," of "relief," "like a weight has been lifted."

With acceptance, your suffering dissipates. The pain doesn't disappear. But because you aren't suffering, the pain becomes more bearable and dissipates over time.

Women often get hung up on the idea of forgiveness during divorce — they cannot bring themselves to forgive a cheating husband who has abandoned them and the kids. Radical acceptance presents an attractive alternative when forgiveness feels impossible. Radical acceptance has nothing to do with the other person. It's completely about reducing your personal pain.

Amy worked with a psychiatrist during her divorce, who told her that in order to move forward, she needed to forgive her husband for having an affair with another woman. Amy wasn't ready to forgive and could not take the necessary steps to end her marriage. She was locked into a cycle of pain and suffering, and she could not let go and move forward with her life. When Amy shifted her focus to accepting that she could move

> WISE WOMEN KNOW
> *"The curious paradox is when I accept myself just as I am, then I can change."*
> — Carl Rogers

forward by practicing radical acceptance, things began to shift for her. She recognized that she could let go of the cycle of pain and yet still hold her ex completely responsible for his behavior.

Radical acceptance takes lots of practice. Understandably, it might feel strange and hard. But remember that radical acceptance is about acknowledging reality — not liking it or contesting it. Once you acknowledge what's really happening, you can change it and start to heal. Radical acceptance has nothing to do with being passive or giving up. To the contrary, it's about channeling your energy into moving on. Follow the steps below to embrace *what is* so that you can move forward and live your life on your terms.

Mindful Action Steps

- **Create a new mind-set:** Instead of resistance, practice acceptance to embrace the things you cannot change. While engaging in your meditation practice, repeat this mantra: *I may not be happy about this result, but I accept it.*

- **Change your perspective:** Outcomes depend heavily on factors beyond our control. Your spouse wants a divorce. You have to share custody of the children. You have to go back to work. Fighting these realities may have a more negative impact on your emotional well-being than the problem itself. Instead, accept these realities and lean into them. Practice this mantra throughout the day when things don't go as planned: *Perhaps there is another way to look at this.*

- **Choose peace of mind:** Accept and move on from your history and how you feel about it. At some point, fighting because you are "right" and have been "wronged" is self-defeating and keeps you stuck. Minimize the self-talk about what *shouldn't have happened* so you can move on. Practice this mantra when the chatter in your head becomes deafening: *I'd rather be at peace than be right.*

- **Allow yourself to process pain:** Accepting the way things are doesn't mean we escape pain. In fact, it can open the door to experiencing necessary mourning because we resist the urge to numb our feelings. Accepting reality gives us the space to work through our feelings effectively. When engaging in your meditation practice each day, allow yourself to feel any discomfort you may be experiencing. Envision a healing golden light encompassing your body and bringing you peace. Breathe that golden light into whatever part of your body is feeling tight or anxious, and experience the relief it brings. Repeat this mantra: *I am safe.*

> WISE WOMEN KNOW
> *You have the power to choose your response. In your response lies your freedom.*

CHAPTER 7

Taking Charge

"The power to change is in my hands."

— Helen M. Ryan

*Y*ou're almost there. Once you have reached agreement with your spouse on all the major issues of your divorce, the last step in the dissolution process is the preparation of the final divorce decree, which will be submitted for the court's approval. And while you may be quite anxious to be done with all the negotiations, there will still be a number of details to resolve and incorporate into the final judgment (the divorce decree). Be aware that this stage includes some last-minute negotiations that require your continued focus (and which this chapter addresses).

Know that the final divorce decree is not the end of your life — it is the beginning of a new and better life. It's totally up to you now. And with great freedom comes newfound responsibility. One realm that newly divorced women sometimes struggle with is managing finances. If you never did this while you were married, you get to do that now. Further, if you were a stay-at-home mom, or only took jobs for extra income, this is your opportunity to develop a meaningful career. This moment is all about stepping out of the frame that has defined you as a married woman and creating the life you choose.

This is not the finish line. It is the starting gate. It is your opportunity to start anew. Do not take your foot off the gas pedal. Press forward and follow these steps to create a new and better reality.

DIVORCE HACKS

 Preparation of the Final Divorce Decree

A stipulated judgment or marital settlement agreement (MSA) contains all the terms of your settlement. Every issue in your divorce, such as custody, support, and division of property, should be addressed in it. This agreement is signed by both parties, attached to a judgment form, and submitted to the court for the judge's signature. Once the judge signs, the divorce decree is binding, and afterward, no changes can be made unless there is a compelling reason, such as that one party has withheld information that would have materially changed the division of assets, there is a material change in circumstances concerning one party's earnings, or there is a substantial change in the parenting plan. Asking a judge to modify a signed, final divorce decree requires an attorney and often substantial fees.

Where both parties have counsel, one spouse's attorney prepares the draft MSA. I recommend that your attorney do this to ensure that the document is drafted with you and your requirements in mind; this is easier than trying to add them to the opposing counsel's MSA.

If you have gone through mediation and neither spouse has retained a lawyer, then the mediator may be retained to prepare the final judgment. Find out in advance whether the mediator will provide this service when you are deciding who to retain to handle the mediation. Self-represented parties can obtain advice from self-help centers, which are usually located at the family law court. However, for complex settlements, it is advisable to have a lawyer draft the final judgment to make certain that you are fully protected.

Be prepared for a lengthy document and for some final negotiations. If your attorney drafts the document, you will need to carefully review it before it is sent to your spouse's attorney. Then, expect that your spouse and his attorney will not agree to every provision and will make suggestions to edit the document. The same is true for you if your spouse's attorney drafts the MSA; expect that you will want to make adjustments to terms and language.

The reasons for these last-minute negotiations is that, in addition to containing everything you and your spouse have agreed to in order to settle all the issues in your divorce, the MSA will include new provisions that are necessary to carry out the spirit and intent of the settlement. These are things you haven't expressly agreed to and which you might want to adjust.

It may go without saying, but you need to carefully read and make sure you understand the entire MSA. Confirm that all the terms you have agreed to are included and that you're comfortable with any additional language. Custody and visitation schedules can be confusing; clean yours up now, if needed, to prevent a later dispute. The MSA will include the details of property distributions. Make certain you understand the tax consequences associated with property division, which may not be spelled out in the MSA. If necessary, consult with your tax professional before you sign the MSA, to make certain you are clear about all the tax implications and there are no surprises.

If certain language doesn't quite match your recollection of the settlement terms, question them. Ask your attorney about every provision not previously discussed. In essence, take the time to ask every question you can think of until you are satisfied that the terms as written are the ones you agree to and that you understand the meaning and implications of every term.

For instance, the terms for child and spousal support are court orders and are enforceable by contempt if they are not complied with. Ask your attorney about enforcement and the consequences for not abiding by what's written. Every provision of your MSA is intended to be binding and enforceable, one way or another.

One issue that can come up now, if it hasn't come up before, is how to divide pension or retirement benefits, which requires requesting a qualified domestic relations order (see below).

Remember: When you sign the final divorce decree, it's binding, so make certain you are clear about what is in it. Your MSA then goes to the court to have the judgment entered. Once that's done, the divorce process is over.

Dividing Retirement Benefits

Retirement plans are often overlooked during divorce proceedings, in part because a divorce can occur years before retirement — and who's thinking about retirement when it's ten or twenty years down the road? Further, pension or retirement benefits are not automatically split during a divorce, so if you don't request that this marital asset be divided, each spouse will keep the entirety of whatever they have. Remember, if a 401K, IRA, or pension is in your husband's name, you own a portion of whatever was earned during marriage. And your husband is entitled to a share of retirement funds you earned during the marriage, even if the fund is in your name.

To divide certain of these benefits, you may need a qualified domestic relations order (QDRO), and it should be addressed in the MSA. A retirement plan can be one of the largest assets in a marriage, and if a divorce is finalized without a QDRO, the former spouse has no rights to their ex's retirement benefits (unless the divorce case is reopened). So request your rightful share, and don't put yourself at risk of economic insecurity in retirement.

What Is a QDRO?

A qualified domestic relations order is a special court order that grants a person a right to a portion of the retirement benefits his or her former spouse has earned through participation in an employer-sponsored retirement plan. A QDRO is required for any retirement plan covered by the Employee Retirement Income Security Act (ERISA). Note that a QDRO is not necessary to divide an individual retirement account (IRA) or a simplified employee pension (SEP).

In a QDRO, the person who earned the benefit is called the "participant," and the person who is designated to receive a share of that benefit is called the "alternate payee." QDROs can award benefits to the alternate payee while the participant is alive, as well as survivor benefits if the participant dies.

In addition, a separate QDRO must be filed for each retirement plan. There are nearly seven hundred thousand private retirement plans in the United States, and each one has its own rules for what information must be included in a QDRO. However, there are basic elements that each QDRO contains: the dollar amount or percentage of the benefit to be paid to the alternate payee, and the number of payments or time period to which the order applies.

Obtaining a QDRO

Preparation of a QDRO is highly technical and must be done correctly or the retirement plan won't accept it. Some attorneys specialize in preparing QDROs and do nothing else. Don't be surprised if, as you reach the end of your divorce, you are required to retain QDRO counsel to divide the retirement assets. If you do, their retainer fee should be substantially less than the one for your divorce attorney. Ask your attorney to negotiate that the fee is either paid by your spouse or split between you. Provision for the QDRO and how it will be paid should be included in the MSA.

Take Control of Your Finances

Once your divorce is final, you can at last get started creating the rest of your life. And in order to make your life the best it can possibly be, you have to get your finances under control. Everyone hates the word *budget*. But what if you could have a new relationship with your money? What if you could take charge of your money so that you could live the life you wish? You can.

> WISE WOMEN KNOW
> *"Money should not dictate how I live my life. I must take charge and become the master of money, so that I decide what I want to do with my time."*
> — Manoj Arora

Instead of cringing at the thought of creating a "budget," think of this as planning for a future where you have the financial freedom to do what you want. You will have to pay your bills, save and invest for your retirement, plan for college if you have children, map out other long-term goals, and plan for the savings and investments you will need to help you achieve it all. Careful and thoughtful investments coupled with living within your means are the keys to making your divorce settlement last

as long as possible and creating income to fund future endeavors.

Consider Karen. She navigated her way through a divorce and successfully pushed the "restart" button on her personal, professional, and financial life — at the age of fifty-four.

In the 1990s, Karen and her then-husband, Bill, founded a San Francisco–based technology firm. Those were heady days for tech start-ups, and the company took off. Karen and Bill traveled frequently and spent money freely. Like many couples, they didn't focus on saving for retirement and investing, assuming the money would continue to roll in. They owned two homes, so when the monthly bills came due, there were two of everything. Their kids went to private schools. Then the dot-com bubble burst, the company failed, and Karen and Bill's marriage crumbled with it.

Through sheer grit and determination, Karen regained control of her finances. What follows are the steps she took to get her financial footing back on solid ground.

Set Spending Guardrails: The 50/30/20 Plan

When she got divorced, the first thing Karen did was set up a budget. She wrote down all her monthly expenses and sources of income. She became aware of how much money she spent on her home, car, and retirement fund. But how did her financial allocation compare to the amount she *ideally* should spend and save? Now that you are on your own, it's never been more important to set guardrails so that you can have the money you need.

Start with the income and expense declaration you prepared during your divorce (see "Preparing Your Financial Disclosures," page 92), which should provide a very clear understanding of what funds are coming in and what funds are going out. Update this postdivorce, so that it reflects the needs of your new household. Make sure to specify all day-to-day expenses — including monthly utilities, any mortgage, car payments, and so on — and all income: from a job, your investments, and any spousal and child support you're now receiving.

Using this accounting, you'll develop a 50/30/20 plan, which creates a blueprint so that you can meet your fixed costs and set aside money for savings and retirement. While you may not be able to follow it precisely, it is a useful rule of thumb that guides spending. Here is that plan in four steps.

STEP 1: CALCULATE YOUR AFTER-TAX INCOME

Your after-tax income is the amount you collect after taxes are taken out of your paycheck, such as state tax, local tax, and Medicare and Social Security tax.

If you're an employee with a paycheck, your after-tax income is easy to figure out. If health care, retirement contributions, or any other deductions are taken out of your paycheck, simply add them back in.

If you're self-employed, your after-tax income equals your gross income minus your business expenses (such as the cost of your laptop, business travel, and so on), and minus the amount you set aside for taxes.

If you receive spousal support and child support, these are included in your income.

STEP 2: LIMIT YOUR NEEDS TO 50 PERCENT

Review your budget. Note how much you spend on "needs" such as groceries, housing, utilities, health insurance, and car insurance. The amount that you spend on these needs should be no more than 50 percent of your total after-tax pay, according to the 50/30/20 percentages.

What's a need and what's a want? That's the million-dollar question. Any payment that you can forgo with only minor inconvenience, like your cable bill or your back-to-school clothing, is a want. Any payment that would severely impact your quality of life, such as electricity and prescription medicines, is a need. If you can't forgo a payment, such as a minimum repayment on a credit card, it is also a need because your credit score will be hurt if you don't pay the minimum.

When Karen evaluated her needs versus wants, she realized that instead of eating out at a restaurant and spending twenty-five dollars for a plate of pasta, she could invite her friends over and ask everyone to bring something.

STEP 3: LIMIT YOUR WANTS TO 30 PERCENT

On the surface, step three sounds great. Thirty percent of my money can be put toward my wants? Hello, beautiful shoes, a trip to Bali, spa treatments, and Italian restaurants.

Wait! Not so fast. Remember the definition of a "need"? Your wants include your unlimited text messaging plan, your home's cable bill, and cosmetic (or nonmechanical) repairs to your car.

Sometimes a need becomes a want by degrees. Bread is a need; Oreo cookies are a want. Yes, they're both food, which is a necessity, but cookies are clearly discretionary.

You may spend more on wants than you think. Again, you need clothing, but how much and what kind? I encourage you to be honest with yourself and qualify anything above the minimum needed as a want. Then shop at discount outlets, not upscale malls, and so on.

Limiting your "wants" will go a long way toward getting you on the right track with your budget. Remember, this doesn't have to be permanent. You are in transition, which won't last forever. If you stay focused on the end goal — financial security and the peace of mind it affords — limiting your wants for the time being will be well worth it.

Step 4: Spend 20 percent on savings and debt repayments

Spend at least 20 percent of your after-tax income repaying debts and saving money in your emergency fund and your retirement accounts.

If you carry a credit card balance, the minimum payment is a "need," which counts toward the 50 percent. Anything beyond that is an additional debt repayment, which qualifies toward this 20 percent. If you carry a mortgage or a car loan, the minimum payment is a need, and any extra payments count toward your 20 percent savings and debt repayment.

Hire a Financial Adviser

Karen got a lump sum of money as part of her divorce settlement, and she knew she needed to invest it somehow. She signed up for a managed account service because she's not very market savvy and felt she needed a guiding hand to help her along. The fee she pays is a percentage of the amount invested. If, like Karen, you are still learning about successful investing and how to move money around, hiring a financial adviser is a worthwhile investment.

In a recent study conducted by Fidelity Investments, less than half of the women surveyed felt confident talking to a professional financial adviser about money and investments. Women tend to think they need gobs of money before they can talk to a financial adviser. However, all of the fundamental components of a sound financial plan should be completed under the guidance of an adviser who is very familiar with the needs and issues of divorced women. When you got divorced, your team of professionals may have included a financial adviser. Use that adviser now to help plan for your future. You want to be able to fund your goals and aspirations as well as plan for retirement, so you don't outlive your money.

If you didn't work with a financial adviser during your divorce, you need one now more than ever. How do you pick a financial adviser? It's important to know two things about your adviser. First, how do they get paid? Do they receive a fee or work on commission? Second, it's key that any adviser you use is a fiduciary, meaning he or she has a legal duty to act in your best interest.

Commission-Based and Fee-Based Financial Planners

Commission-based financial planners are often agents or brokers who make a commission off of selling financial products, like an insurance policy or mutual fund. Because of that, they may be incentivized to sell a specific product to their clients.

Fee-based financial planners are essentially also commission-based financial planners operating under a different name. They charge a fee for their financial advice in addition to earning a commission from the product they are selling.

Fiduciaries and Fee-Only Financial Planners

Fee-only financial planners only sell financial advice. They are usually registered investment advisers, or fiduciaries, meaning they have a fiduciary responsibility to act in their clients' best interest. Fee-only financial planners are also generally not incentivized to sell you a specific product, as they usually do not earn a commission.

Fee-only financial planner rates can vary. Some planners may charge a percentage of their client's assets. These planners will often only work with clients with a high net worth because their compensation is directly related to the size of their clients' portfolios. Because they're incentivized to make their clients more money, these planners tend to focus on investment advice.

Other fee-only financial planners may charge an hourly rate, flat fee, or annual retainer. While their advice is likely to be the most holistic, the cost may be high. Many fee-only financial planners can often range from $1,000 to $3,000 or more annually.

UNDERSTANDING FINANCIAL PLANNER CERTIFICATIONS

What about certifications? Certified Financial Planners (CFPs) are bound by the CFP board's rules of conduct, which provide that a CFP owes the client the duty of care of a fiduciary when providing financial planning. CFPs are qualified to advise you on almost any question about your financial situation, such as how to gain control over your budget, what kind of insurance you need, how to make sure your investment portfolio reflects your long-term goals, and how to address your estate planning needs. Every CFP has completed courses on topics like insurance, estate planning, retirement, taxes, and investing; passed the CFP board's ethical requirements; and undergone a ten-hour, 285-question exam. In addition, he or she must have at least three years of job experience in the financial planning industry or a two-year apprenticeship under a CFP. While many other designations mean someone is an expert in a particular area like taxes or insurance, the CFP designation is the most all-encompassing.

Connect with a professional through the databases of the National Association of Personal Financial Advisors (www.napfa.org), the Financial Planning Association (www.plannersearch.org), or the Certified Financial Planner Board of Standards (www.cfp.net).

Investments and Retirement

Still today, Karen doesn't have a job with a 401K, but she contributes a portion of her alimony to an IRA each month. Then she makes an additional $1,000 contribution as a "catch-up" because she's over fifty. Karen has made funding her IRA a priority since her divorce. To get started, she set up an auto-deduction of $500 from her checking account every month. And she really doesn't miss it. It's money she would have spent on who knows what.

Typically, most divorces strike when people are older. Among US adults ages fifty and older, the "gray divorce" rate has roughly doubled since the 1990s. In these cases, it's more important than ever to make certain that your investments are properly aligned with the specific time frames of your goals.

- Do you need the money in one or two years? Short-term investments are appropriate, like money markets, CDs, and saving accounts.
- Do you need the money in two to three years? Seek lower-risk investments, such as short-term bonds.
- Do you need the money in four to five years? You can add some stocks (or risk investments) into the portfolio.
- Do you have long-term goals? Weigh the portion of your assets assigned to that goal toward risk assets (like stocks).
- Do you need assets to fund daily and annual living expenses? The way this is invested will depend on how much you spend, how long you need the assets to last (your age), and many other considerations, such as your employment situation and tolerance for risk.

Ramp Up Your Money Smarts

For Karen, educating herself about her finances and investing has been her biggest challenge. During her marriage, she relied on her husband to manage their investments. Now she wants to understand how the market works so she can feel more confident about how to invest. She started reading about investing topics by subscribing to *Money* magazine. She studies her bank and brokerage statements carefully, so she really understands them. And she regularly checks in with her financial adviser and isn't afraid to ask questions as she climbs the learning curve about her investments.

When reviewing your monthly statements, here is what to look for:

- Are there any unusual withdrawals?
- Has the portfolio grown from one month to the next? Learn about the S&P 500 index. Most portfolios are less aggressive than that index, so you shouldn't expect to match it, but be aware of how your growth compares to it. Your adviser may create a "blended" index for better comparison.
- Is the portfolio down when the index is up? Be aware that this can happen, but understand why. Did you forget about withdrawals you made? Is the portfolio too conservative? Too aggressive? Not diversified enough? Talk to your adviser.

Recommended Resources for Taking Control of Your Finances

To further your financial education, there are a wealth of resources in print and online. Here are a few suggestions to get you started.

- Carrie Schwab-Pomerantz, *The Charles Schwab Guide to Finances After Fifty* (New York: Crown Business, 2014): Drawing on thirty years of financial experience, questions from her syndicated "Ask Carrie" column, and the latest guidance from the Schwab Center for Financial Research, Carrie Schwab-Pomerantz tackles today's complex challenges and offers clear, straightforward advice.

- Eleanor Blayney, *Women's Worth: Finding Your Financial Confidence* (Virginia: Direction$, 2010): Certified Financial Planner Eleanor Blayney breaks through the traditionally male-dominated field of financial advice to offer information that you as a woman can really use. Her frank approach intersperses practical advice with easy-to-do exercises that will help you understand your beliefs about money, learn the fundamentals of financial planning, and gain confidence in your financial know-how.

- Smart About Money (www.smartaboutmoney.org): This program of the National Endowment for Financial Education includes online courses and tools such as "Budget Wizard" and financial calculators that determine how long it will take to pay off credit card debt and whether to purchase or lease an auto.

- Women's Institute for a Secure Retirement (WISER, www.wiserwomen.org): The Women's Institute for a Secure Retirement recently published a new downloadable edition of its guide, *Divorce and Retirement: How to Take Control of Retirement Benefits*. This short, commonsense guide emphasizes the importance of retirement benefits in a divorce and offers valuable information on marital property, negotiating an agreement, and getting a qualified domestic relations order (QDRO).

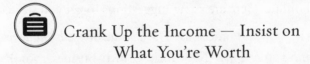 Crank Up the Income — Insist on What You're Worth

Now that your divorce is final and support has been decided, it's time to crank up your income. While you may have been incentivized to minimize your income to maximize the support you receive (or to minimize what you have to pay), now you can go for it.

If you want to get paid what you're worth, you have to be willing to ask for it. Whether you work for a large company or for yourself, it's all about "the ask." And "the ask" is all about your self-worth.

If You're an Employee: Asking for a Raise

Women, on average, earn eighty cents for every dollar that men earn. Some of the pay gap stems from the concentration of women in low-paying industries and occupations. But much of it is because women underestimate their skill set and what they're worth. We take what we're given and don't think about asking for what we're worth. If you're an employee, the only way to increase your income is to ask for a raise (or find a new job that pays better).

FIGURE OUT WHAT YOU'RE WORTH, IN YOUR COMPANY AND THE INDUSTRY

First, find out how your salary compares to that paid for the same position by other companies and across your industry. To find out what employers are paying other people with the same job title, check out Salary.com or PayScale (www.payscale.com). The website Glassdoor (www.glassdoor.com) has a tool called "Know Your Worth" that calculates your market worth based on your employer, location, education, years of experience, and other details.

Then, quantify why you deserve a raise in your company for the job you already do. Create a list with two columns. List all the things you were hired for on the left, and list all the things you currently do on the right. You don't get a raise for working hard. You get a raise when you prove your job has grown, and you are contributing significantly more to the company.

Finally, don't just name what you do, quantify your impact. As much as you can, back up your request with data that shows your performance merits giving you what you want. This is easier when you have a revenue-generating job with clear metrics of success. But many women in support or operational roles can come up with clear, quantifiable measures to track their performance. Show how much you improve the bottom line.

CHOOSE YOUR MOMENT AND NEGOTIATE EFFECTIVELY

Don't just pop into your boss's office to demand a raise. Catching someone off guard to talk about money is never a good idea. Plan to talk over lunch or schedule a time. Pick a time of day when things quiet down — typically end of day.

Then, negotiating is much more effective when you focus on the needs and interests of the other side, rather than on your own. Show how you solve problems or how you help your boss achieve their goals, whether for the department or the coming year. Find out what those goals are if you don't know. People pay money to those who can solve their problems or decrease their workload.

Finally, remember that this is a financial transaction, not a statement of how much your boss likes you. Don't personalize it; this isn't about whether you are doing a good job. Assume you are doing a good job or you wouldn't still be there. A raise is based on available money and budgets. Men are very good at using a matter-of-fact tone when negotiating their pay — it's not emotional for them. It's "business." Women are taught to be "nice." Steal from men's playbook on this one and keep emotion out of it.

> WISE WOMEN KNOW
> "Taking risks, choosing growth, challenging ourselves, and asking for promotions (with smiles on our faces, of course) are all important elements of managing a career. One of my favorite quotes comes from author Alice Walker, who observed, 'The most common way people give up their power is by thinking they don't have any.' Do not wait for power to be offered. Like that tiara, it might never materialize. And anyway, who wears a tiara on a jungle gym?"
> — Sheryl Sandberg

NEGOTIATE FOR MORE THAN JUST PAY

Your long-term satisfaction in a job is dependent on many things, not just salary. There are multiple "levers" you can pull as you negotiate — such as salary, bonuses, perks, assignments, or flex time. What, besides more money, would improve your life? Provide options, which gives your employer the opportunity to work with you rather than just say yes or no. If you are asking for significantly more money, give your boss the option to do half now and half in six months. Getting money approved is never easy, so a "creative budgeting" suggestion will be appreciated.

If You're Self-Employed: Increasing Your Income

If you work for yourself, one of the best ways to increase your revenue is to raise your rates. Here again, it's all about "the ask." Many women struggle with asking for more. You're used to valuing yourself at a certain level, and when you think about asking for more, uncertainty floods in: *What if they say no and take their business elsewhere?* All too often, women will underquote out of fear. Even though they're attracting clients, they're still losing a lot of potential revenue because they're being underpaid.

When setting your prices, chances are you're asking the wrong questions. Don't ask: "What are my clients willing to pay?" and "What is my competition charging?" Instead, ask, "How much money would make this job worth my time?"

This can be uncomfortable, especially if you feel raising your rates will scare off potential clients. But you have to do it if you want to make what you're worth. Remember, it isn't just about the effort you put into the job. It's about the benefit that your work gives to your clients.

What if the value you're offering seems like less than the price you want to charge? Do not drop your rates — instead, raise your value.

For example, Rachel was hired to help one of her clients with her social media marketing. The client needed help with her Facebook page for her business. She wanted Rachel to rework it so that it would better reflect her story and her passion.

Rachel wanted to do more than just rewrite her client's Facebook page. She wanted to rework all of her social media to reflect her brand. She put together a proposal to do just that and quoted a price reflecting this value. While the quote was significantly more than the client had initially agreed to pay, she quickly understood the value Rachel offered and agreed to pay her what she asked. Rachel doubled her income with that particular client by giving her real value for the money.

Decide right now that you will do the following things to increase your value and your earnings if you work for yourself. Here are the three main things to keep in mind:

- Charge at the top of your field, not the bottom: If your rates are comparatively low, potential clients will just assume you aren't as good as your competitors. Charge more than the competition, and people will assume you are better. It's like buying a designer blouse. People assume it's special or better because it costs more.
- Increase your rate with new clients: If you don't want to charge your current clients more, then raise your rates with new clients. They will pay it, which will increase your confidence, and you will set a new benchmark for what you charge.
- Raise your value to justify higher rates: What do your clients want and need? If you can fulfill an unmet need, abundance will naturally follow.

 How to Handle the New Girlfriend

Your divorce is final and you and your ex are implementing the parenting plan. You are finding a "new normal" with your kids and reestablishing positive relationships among everyone. It's not perfect, but in some ways you're getting along better than ever with your ex, and then "it" happens: He's got a girlfriend, and he wants your children to meet her. Now what? Will the children remain his priority? Will the girlfriend treat them well? Will you be replaced?

It's natural to feel threatened and have doubts, so keep the following things in mind. It's also worth remembering that if (or when) you begin dating, some of these same issues may apply to you (see also "Dating During Divorce," page 119).

Be Secure in Your Relationship with Your Child

If you're doing what you're supposed to in order to build a bond and influence your children to be the best they can be, relax and keep being the best mom you can be. No one can replace you — full stop. You are Mom. This is one job where you truly are irreplaceable.

Be Reliable: Turn Disruptions into Opportunities

Typically, when an ex-husband gets a new girlfriend, she becomes his priority, not the kids, at least temporarily. Your ex may suddenly be as reliable as a seventeen-year-old boy. He might become unavailable for his scheduled visitation because he's spending time with her. This can be frustrating and disruptive. However, if you view this as an opportunity to spend more time with your children and strengthen your bond, both you and your kids will be the winners. Rather than insisting on enforcing the parenting schedule, be flexible and take the children if you can. What you don't want to do is force your ex to take the kids if he really doesn't want to. Nothing good will come from that.

Be patient — this stage will pass, and if you handle it well, both you and the kids can actually benefit. Your kids will learn that they can rely on you, and in the end, your relationship with them will be strengthened. At some point, the kids will be old enough to choose for themselves who they spend time with. If you are there for them when they need you, you make it easy for them to choose you.

Let Kids Make Their Own Judgments

So, what if he's taking her on expensive trips and to fancy restaurants, while he's feeding the kids McDonalds? What can you do? Nothing. I know — it's not fair. But recognize that this won't last forever. As long as he is making his child support payments and not engaging in abusive behavior, let small injustices go. Most of all, avoid the temptation to point out this behavior to your kids. They will figure out what's going on — and it's very hard for them when they recognize that they are not their father's priority. This is why it is so important that they know that they are your priority.

Be Watchful: Take Action When Necessary

That said, don't be hands-off when you see behavior that is explicitly harmful or abusive. For instance, if you know your ex and his girlfriend abuse alcohol or drugs, or engage in any other abusive, neglectful behavior that harms the children, then seek a change in custody and the parenting plan. These instances are rare, but I have had to go to court on occasion to obtain a new custody arrangement when the new girlfriend has created serious problems that impact the children. If your child's health, welfare, or safety are threatened, it's time to call your attorney and take action.

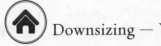 Downsizing — When Less Is More

If you decided to sell your family home during the divorce, and are now preparing to follow through and sell it, you have done yourself a huge favor. We tend to cling to what we have longer than is helpful. I did. I convinced myself that staying in the family home was best for the kids. But in reality, leaving and starting over was what we needed. For me, letting go of the single biggest symbol of our marriage — the family home — was one of the hardest parts of getting divorced, but it was also one of the greatest gifts.

However, whether you're selling your home or staying, you have a great opportunity: It gives you the chance to downsize, to clean out all the clutter and old memories. Even if you are staying in your family home, consider decluttering your old life as if you were moving so that you can start fresh.

After my divorce, I rented a home half the size of our family home. The smaller house brought me and the kids closer together. That time spent in close quarters served each of us well as we moved through the early days of the divorce. Now that my kids are teenagers, I can see that the time we spent in that smaller house helped us create a bond that continues to this day.

Moving to a much smaller house forced us to simplify our existence, which was tremendously beneficial. We let go of a lot of stuff we didn't need and learned we could get by with much less. We learned the difference between wants and needs as we cut our belongings in half. These lessons continue to serve us.

Renting was a gift. No property taxes. When something broke, I could call the landlord. Utilities were about half what they were before. And minimizing maintenance and expenses freed up time and money for things that really mattered while our lives were in transition.

What I learned about letting go of the family home and downsizing was that the very thing I feared the most was exactly what I needed to re-create my life in a new and better way.

Here are the steps to take in order to eliminate the old and make way for the new.

Get Rid of Everything You Don't Need

The treadmill that's been gathering dust. Those Jimmy Choos that haven't seen action in years. Those jeans that no longer fit. Do you really need any of that stuff in your new home? In your new life?

Whether or not you are moving, take a good long look at everything you own and how you live your life daily. Then, get rid of all the things that aren't *already a part of* your actual lifestyle. Don't keep things that you *want* or *hope* to be part of your lifestyle. Keep only what you actually need for who you are right now.

As you gather items to get rid of, put them for now in boxes, crates, or bags and store them in a garage or other area. Then see the next section below.

- Take a walk through your house or apartment and evaluate everything you come across (furniture, books, food, and so on). Ask yourself whether you've used it in the past year, and if so, how often. Be honest with yourself. If you think you could live well without it, out the door it should go. Keep a list of items to get rid of, if that helps.

- Go through your main storage areas (your attic, basement, and garage). You will be surprised at everything you've stashed away. If you're like most people, you will find boxes of items that haven't seen the light of day for years, and there's a reason: You don't need them. Get rid of them at once.

- Get rid of anything that's a tribute to an unmet goal. The prime example is the exercise machine. We always say we'll use it, but then we don't. Be ruthless and include books waiting to be read, furniture you mean to fix up, and anything you're holding on to "just in case," hoping that the presence of the object will inspire its use. Be realistic. Get rid of whatever is coated in dust to make room for the things you'll actually use.

- One at a time, clear out every cabinet, shelf, and closet till they're empty. Then only put back the things you can't live well without. That means that if you use a whisk every other day, it stays. But the melon baller you never use, since you don't even like melon — out it goes.

- Don't forget to go through your bathroom cabinets, kitchen pantry, and "junk" drawers. We have a tendency to accumulate unnecessary items in these places. Get rid of empty bottles, balls of twine, expired medicines, dried-up beauty products, and your collection of plastic margarine containers. Be brutal.

- For rarely used stuff that you really have a hard time getting rid of, make this agreement with yourself: Put the items in the garage. If you don't need or use them within six months, give, sell, or throw them away.

Trash, Donate, Give Away, or Sell

How you dispose of unnecessary items will depend on what they are, how much you care about them, and how much energy and time you have. Many things will go right in the trash, but what about things that are still in good shape, that *somebody* could use? You can either give them away or sell them.

Here are ways to give stuff away:

- The easiest thing to do is to load them up in your car and drop them off at the nearest thrift shop. Some places that take donations will schedule a pickup for large items and quantities.

- Join a Freecycle group to give stuff away (www.free cycle.org).

- If you live in an apartment building or townhouse complex, see if there is a noticeboard or drop-off area for giving away unwanted items.

- Call up your friends and relatives and see if they want anything. Trade your unwanted furniture for their help during your move to your new place!

Who couldn't use a premove windfall? If you want to make some cash, try these selling strategies:

- Have a yard sale (or two), or consider a service to take care of it for you (search online for "liquidation estate content sales").
- If you have time, utilize websites such as Craigslist and eBay to sell off the best stuff. You'll likely get more money for your items this way, but it is more time-consuming.
- Craigslist is a good avenue for selling larger items such as furniture, appliances, and home décor items to people living in your area. If you can, offering delivery will often produce quicker sales.
- eBay is a good venue for selling collectible items, such as old albums, comic books, and figurines. Make sure to take high-quality photos of the items and provide good descriptions. Remember that you are a salesperson. Sell those products!
- Used designer clothing can be resold in consignment shops. Search your local business directory, and be sure to shop around. Some stores offer better rates than others.

Planning and Packing for Your Move

Once you've weeded out all the stuff you don't need, you can prepare to move into your new space. In essence, you need to make sure that everything you intend to bring will fit in the new space, and then pack everything up so you can find it easily when you unpack.

MEASURE YOUR FURNITURE AND MAKE SURE EVERYTHING FITS

You will need to know whether your furniture will fit into your new space — particularly large items such as your sofa and your bed — so measure everything.

Then, take measurements of every room, or get a floor plan if one is available. Using these dimensions and measurements, consider furniture placement in each room, and don't forget about the location of doors and windows. Try using *Better Homes & Gardens'* Arrange-a-Room online software to simplify the process (requires registration but is free; www.bhg.com/decorating/arrange -a-room). This will give you a much better idea of what you can keep and what will have to go.

Assess your new storage areas

Sure, you've gotten rid of a lot of stuff, but is it enough? How much storage does your new place have? Will you have fewer kitchen cupboards? How many closets are there? If you are moving into an apartment, does it have a storage locker, and if so, what are its dimensions?

If you're worried that everything you have won't fit, get rid of more stuff or plan for other storage options. In addition, consider whether the new place configures storage areas and cabinets differently. For example, will the kitchen cabinets in your new place hold all the things your cabinets do in your current home?

Pack up in an organized way

Label every box by room. Keep a list if you need to. Don't think that you will remember that the big television box is actually full of pots and pans. You won't.

For items that will remain in storage (winter clothes, holiday decorations, etc.), pack them in the same containers you will keep them in. I recommend see-through plastic storage bins, which come in many sizes, are stackable, and make finding what you need a snap. Color-code plastic storage bins by function to make it easier to locate what you need. Use measurements of the new storage areas to ensure a good fit. Come moving day, these bins will be easy to deal with.

Moving into Your New Home

In addition to enlisting a moving crew of friends and family to help, here are tips to make moving day as easy as possible.

MOVE LARGE ITEMS FIRST

Move your furniture into your new home first. You will have the most energy for this task at the beginning, and it will also give you a better indication of where the smaller things will go. Do not merely fill a room with furniture and plan to sort it all out later. There is nothing worse than trying to navigate through small rooms littered with boxes and stacks of furniture after a day of moving. Place furniture in the rooms as you go, according to your plan.

PUT AWAY STORAGE ITEMS

Contained items that are meant for storage can be placed directly in their allotted spaces where they will be out of the way. By putting these things away as you move in, you save yourself the stress of trying to maneuver through jam-packed rooms during the next few days.

ORGANIZE AS YOU UNPACK

Put labeled boxes in their respective rooms. That way, you know that everything you unpack belongs in that room. I suggest unpacking the bathroom first, as that room is usually needed soonest. If you have kept only the basics, unpacking this room will be a breeze.

Then, utilize closet and cupboard storage solutions as you unpack. This way, more can be stored in these tight spaces, and you will be setting a precedent for how your new, smaller space will be used.

RELAX AND ENJOY!

You have now crossed the threshold to your new life. You no longer have to worry about the financial burden or time-draining tasks of maintaining a home too big for your needs. You have also simplified your life by surrounding yourself with only those things that are most important to you. Rejoice!

 Grit — Essential for Success

Studies have revealed the defining characteristic that sets apart successful people: grit. What is grit? The ability to get up again and again when things don't go according to plan. Teddy Roosevelt summed it up in an address he made at the Sorbonne in 1910:

> It is not the critic who counts; not the man who points out how the strong man stumbles, or where the doer of deeds could have done them better. The credit belongs to the man who is actually in the arena, whose face is marred by dust and sweat and blood; who strives valiantly; who errs, who comes short again and again, because there is no effort without error and shortcoming; but who does actually strive to do the deeds; who knows great enthusiasms, the great devotions; who spends himself in a worthy cause; who at the best knows in the end the triumph of high achievement, and who at the worst, if he fails, at least fails while daring greatly, so that his place shall never be with those cold and timid souls who neither know victory nor defeat.

As you step out of your comfort zone to re-create yourself, the characteristics of the gritty will serve you well. Embracing these attributes will enable you to face challenges and have the tenacity to carry on.

Manage Fear of Failure

Your ability to manage fear of failure is imperative and a predictor of success. The supremely gritty are not afraid to tank, but rather embrace it as part of the process. They understand that there are valuable lessons in defeat and that the vulnerability of perseverance is requisite for high achievement.

Fear of failure can become a debilitating disorder defined by an unhealthy aversion to risk (or a strong resistance to embracing vulnerability). Some symptoms include anxiety, mental blocks, and perfectionism. However, fear can be overcome. The problem is not insurmountable. To overcome fear, you must confront and then go through whatever it is that frightens you. As you confront your fears and take steps to do what is required, your confidence will grow, your courage will increase, and you will fuel your grit.

Go for It

The truly successful individual does more than just work hard — there is an "x factor." She's not afraid to "go for it!" Not content with just showing up, she's not afraid to step out of her comfort zone when a challenge presents itself, as compared to those dependable folks who are more self-controlled and conventional. In other words, in the context of grit and success, it is important to commit to go for the gold rather than just show up for practice.

> WISE WOMEN KNOW
> *"Do something that scares you every day."*
> — Eleanor Roosevelt

Follow Through

Perseverance + long-term goals = grit. The experts agree that goals coupled with lots of practice lead to extraordinary success.

Linda went through a gut-wrenching divorce at the age of fifty-seven and realized that she no longer wanted to work at her marketing job. She wanted to help families going through divorce avoid the pitfalls she experienced. She decided to go back to school to become a licensed marriage and family therapist. To do that, she had to make the long-term goal to go back to school and then stick with it through her internship. She sold her home to pay for her education and to set up her practice. She went through a major downsize to accomplish her dream. Now she is helping others and has her own private practice. Her passion and perseverance led to fulfillment of her goal.

Long-term goals provide the context and framework in which to find the meaning and value of your long-term efforts, which helps cultivate drive, sustainability, passion, courage, stamina...grit.

Have Resilience

As you step out of your comfort zone to face new challenges, you're going to stumble, and you must get back up. Thomas Edison is said to have made a thousand unsuccessful attempts at inventing the light bulb before it worked. The difference between those who are successful and everyone else is that they don't give up. But what is it that gives you the strength to get up, wipe the dust off, and carry on? Resilience.

Resilience is the ability to maintain your purpose despite setbacks. Never is this more important than when you are reinventing yourself after a divorce.

Resilience is a dynamic combination of optimism, creativity, and confidence, which together empower you to reappraise situations and regulate your response. The truly gritty are not discouraged by failure along the way — they understand that it is simply part of the process. Your beliefs provide the power supply for grit. Know that you have a purpose and that you can choose your life's direction. Understand that when things don't go your way, it may be for your best and highest good.

> WISE WOMEN KNOW
> *"Grit is living life like it's a marathon, not a sprint."*
> — Angela Duckworth

Strive for Excellence, Not Perfection

In general, gritty people don't seek perfection, but instead strive for excellence. It may seem that these two have only subtle semantic distinctions, but in fact, they are at odds. Perfection is unforgiving, inflexible, and often unattainable. Anxiety, low self-esteem, clinical depression, obsessive-compulsive disorder, and substance abuse are only a few of the conditions ascribed to "perfectionism." While your life is in transition, it is essential that you let go of the notion that things must be perfect.

Striving for excellence, on the other hand, is an attitude that will serve you well. It is not an end result, but how you approach things. It is far more forgiving, allowing and embracing failure and vulnerability in the ongoing quest for improvement. It allows for disappointment, and it prioritizes progress over perfection. Excellence is closely aligned with grit — which is an attitude about seeking, striving, and never yielding on your quest for fulfillment.

Mindful Action Steps for Cultivating Grit

FIND YOUR PURPOSE

How can you make a lasting contribution by using your skills, talents, and life experience? Journal, meditate, and brainstorm to discover your purpose and how you can reach it. Walk with a trusted friend in the woods, around the block, or on the beach and talk it out. Those who know you well can be a good sounding board for your ideas.

MAKE A PLAN

The shortest distance between two points is a straight line. Map out the path to reach your goal. Do you need additional school or training to accomplish your objective? Do you need additional funding to make it happen? Create an action plan and seek out help if necessary.

GO FOR IT

You've got the good idea, you've come up with a plan, and then — you equivocate. It's natural to bargain with yourself as you step outside your comfort zone. Your rational mind is telling you not to take a risk, to play it safe. Remember, no guts — no glory. Successful people go for it!

SEEK A PARTNER TO HELP STICK WITH IT

Seek out someone else who is starting over and work with them like you would an exercise partner — the partner who waits for you at 6 AM on the corner for your morning run. Make certain that they are gritty — you need a partner who has broken out of their comfort zone and has the willpower to succeed. Meet with this person regularly to discuss where you are on your paths. Provide encouragement and redirection if one of you gets stuck. Sometimes you just need a pep talk to keep you going.

While starting and then growing my law practice, I often questioned whether I was on the right path. I consulted regularly with a trusted friend who was also starting her own business during midlife after her divorce. Using each other as a sounding board was tremendously helpful for both of us. Sometimes, just hearing yourself talk about a perceived problem clarifies the situation and a solution will emerge. Having these discussions allowed me to look at things from a different angle — and sometimes that is just what you need to put things into perspective.

JUST DO IT

Jump in. There is no substitute for action. Don't allow yourself to get stuck because a situation is not perfect or you're not ready. The first prototype for the iPhone barely worked. But it embodied a bold new idea that changed everything. You've got to start somewhere. Take action. And remember — regardless of the outcome, if you step outside your comfort zone, you have succeeded. You have exercised those muscles that increase your courage and confidence — and you cannot fail if you dare greatly.

Recommended Resources for Grit

- Angela Duckworth, "Grit: The Power of Passion and Perseverance," TED Talk (April 2013, www.ted.com/talks /angela_lee_duckworth_grit_the_power_of_passion _and_perseverance): In this illuminating TED Talk, psychologist Angela Duckworth discusses the essential ingredient for success: mental resilience or grit.
- Angela Duckworth, *Grit: The Power of Passion and Perseverance* (New York: Scribner, 2016): In this *New York Times* bestseller, Duckworth reveals how grit defines success and how we can build it.
- Ann Marie Healy and Andrew Zolli, *Resilience: Why Things Bounce Back* (New York: Simon & Schuster, 2013): This book sheds light on how to bounce back in the face of disruption.

CHAPTER 8

Moving Forward

"In the end these things matter most: How well did you love? How fully did you live? How deeply did you learn to let go?"

— Jack Kornfield

*G*etting to this point has truly been a rebirth — which is never easy. It takes great courage and strength to leave the known and venture into the unknown. Having taken the brave steps to finalize your divorce, now you stand on the precipice of your new life. It's time to live the life you choose on your terms.

Naturally, the responsibilities of being on your own may seem daunting at first, but I assure you: *You can do it!* Take it step-by-step, learning as you go, and you will find that it's empowering to make the decisions and be the one who's in control of your future.

I know. Not long ago I was in your shoes — starting from scratch with three children, on my own, not knowing where to turn. Through a financial downturn and my divorce, I lost everything — except my will to survive. As I put my life back together, I learned how liberating it is to be in charge of my future and to create the life I choose.

I now run a business helping women take back their power in the midst of divorce. I experienced a miraculous transformation when I divorced. I learned that life could be much better on my own. If you have been in a marriage that is unsatisfying, you, too, will find that you are happier and healthier once you have untied the knot. I watch virtually all of my clients go through a miraculous transition as we unwind the ties that bind them. It is as though they are awaking from a deep sleep as they find themselves and the freedom to live on their own terms.

You can do this, too, if you follow these strategic steps.

Clearly, your life after divorce will be different than it was before; it will be different than you imagined back when you were just starting out in a new marriage. And yet, adapting to and embracing these changes will ensure your success.

DIVORCE HACKS

Finalize the Paperwork and Organize Your Affairs

Once your divorce settlement agreement is finalized, there is still work to do. Depending on the status of your bank and credit card accounts, your health insurance, and any property, you may still have paperwork to handle. Before your transition from married to single is complete, you must organize your affairs and do the following.

MAKE COPIES OF YOUR CERTIFIED DIVORCE DECREE

Treat your certified divorce decree like all your other important legal documents, such as your birth certificate or passport. Make extra copies, and store them in a secure location. You will need this document in the event you have to go to court to enforce or modify provisions, such as transferring property titles, changing beneficiaries, and so on. You may also need it to obtain new health insurance.

Issues often arise with implementation of the parenting plan and reimbursement of expenses for the children's extracurricular activities and health care — so you will want to have a copy handy for quick reference.

GET YOUR OWN HEALTH INSURANCE

If you already have your own health insurance through your employer, then you're fine. Your current health insurance can stay intact. But if, while married, you were covered under your ex's employer-sponsored group insurance plan, then you need to find your own policy following the divorce — unless your settlement allows for continuation of coverage.

After your divorce, if you find yourself uninsured, you have a few choices:

- Keep your ex-spouse's coverage for a limited time (up to thirty-six months) through COBRA (officially the Consolidated Omnibus Budget Reconciliation Act).
- Find your own insurance policy. Open enrollment for health insurance only occurs at the end of the year, but since you lost (or must change) coverage due to divorce, you qualify for a "special enrollment period," which allows you to enroll without waiting.
- Start new coverage with your employer. Like open enrollment, your divorce qualifies you to sign up for coverage even if it's outside your workplace's enrollment period.

FINALIZE THE TITLE TRANSFER FOR ANY PROPERTY

The divorce decree states which spouse gets what property — such as real estate, automobiles, boats, and so on — but you must both complete the documents that actually transfer the titles to that property. So, complete these transfers by signing and obtaining the necessary documents for items that are being transferred to you, and do the same for items being transferred to your former spouse. Real estate transfers will need to be recorded, which can be done by your attorney. Auto and boat transfers can be done between you and your ex-spouse. For example, in California, both parties sign the "pink slip" in order to transfer title.

ESTABLISH A SYSTEM TO TRACK SUPPORT, ALIMONY, AND SHARED EXPENSES

After divorce, you will most likely remain financially linked with your ex, through support or alimony payments and possibly shared expenses (such as medical bills) for your children. Set up a system to keep track of all this. As I've said, I recommend using a program such as Our Family Wizard (www.ourfamilywizard.com), which many courts order litigants to use to create a system for support ordered and received. Our Family Wizard offers divorced parents an array of tools to easily manage expenses as well as create an accurate, clear log of support received.

As for paying and/or receiving child support, spousal support, and alimony, I suggest establishing direct deposit or income withholding. With direct deposit, you don't have to wait for a check to arrive in the mail. Your attorney can help you establish a wage garnishment if your ex is a W-2 employee. A wage-garnishment order will automatically deposit court-ordered support into your bank account on a regular basis. Conversely, if you are paying support, it's easier all around for this to occur automatically.

CLOSE ANY JOINT ACCOUNTS

You can close joint bank accounts without your spouse's signature. As for credit cards, you need to zero out the balance before they can be closed. If you agreed in your divorce decree to split a balance owed, you can each transfer your half to a card in your name, and then close the account.

UPDATE ALL ACCOUNTS WITH THE CORRECT NAMES

First, if you changed your name as a result of the divorce, you need to change your married name on the following important documents:

- **Your Social Security card:** In order to get a correct Social Security card, you must provide documented proof of US citizenship or residency (a birth certificate or green card), your legal name change (a divorce decree), and your identity (a driver's license or passport). You can do this at a local Social Security Administration office or by mail.
- **Your driver's license:** You can change your name on your driver's license at your local DMV or online. With the application, you must provide proof of your legal name change, surrender your old driver's license, and pay a small fee. You don't have to retake your driving test.
- **Your passport:** You can submit the appropriate forms by mail (find them online at www.travel.state.gov), and include your name change document, a color passport photo, and all applicable fees.
- **Your credit cards:** Some companies allow a name change with a phone call; some require a request in writing.

Second, you need to add your new name to all other accounts, while also removing your ex-husband's name and updating your address if you've moved. Review all of the following:

- Bank, brokerage, and investment accounts
- Employer's records
- IRS records
- Life, health, homeowner's, and disability insurance policies
- Post office (and don't forget to have your mail forwarded if you are moving)
- Professional licenses

- Utility bills
- Children's school(s)

Finally, update the beneficiaries on any accounts or plans that list them, such as:

- Life insurance
- 401Ks
- Pensions
- IRA accounts

 ## How to Avoid Ending Up Back in Court

There are basically two reasons that divorced couples wind up back in court. Either one person is not meeting the obligations of the original divorce decree or, since the decree was finalized, there have been material and substantial changes in circumstances that have led one person to want to change the agreement. What sort of changes? Usually, either one person is now making significantly more money (and the other wants to adjust support) or one person has become neglectful and abusive to the children (and the other wants to adjust custody or deny visitation). In all these cases, it is possible for you or your ex-spouse to go back to court to enforce your divorce decree or modify certain aspects of it.

That said, be cautious about running into court each time your ex-husband is late picking up the kids or gets a raise. You can spend thousands of dollars on motions to modify a divorce decree, and the return on your investment is often not worth it unless there are really good reasons to seek modification.

For instance, I once represented a woman who insisted on filing a motion to modify a divorce decree because her son's school time changed from 8 AM to 9 AM; she wanted to change the holiday schedule so that she would have Christmas Day; and her ex-husband had failed to pay $178 in unreimbursed medical expenses. I explained to her that, in addition to costing more than it was worth, her motion did not meet the legal standard for securing a change, but she insisted on going to court as a "matter of principle," essentially because her ex was a "flake."

I can assure you that virtually every ex is a "flake" when it comes to meeting every detail of their court-ordered obligations and that the only people who come out ahead in proceedings to try to correct that defect are the attorneys.

Modifying or Enforcing a Divorce Decree

Here's how the process works. If one person wants to modify the original divorce decree but the other does not, the process begins by filing a motion for modification with the court that issued the original decree. The motion must then be personally served on the other party.

After the motion is served, the other party typically has a matter of days or weeks in which to file a response, after which a hearing is held. If you want a modification, it's up to you to present proof of the change in circumstances that warrants the modification. If the motion is to modify custody, child support, or visitation, you must also present evidence to show the court why the modification is in the best interests of the children.

If your goal is to enforce the original decree because your ex-spouse is failing to comply with it, you file a motion for contempt and seek enforcement of its terms. Failure of the other spouse to comply after being held in contempt of the original decree can result in criminal charges, fines, or jail time. Sometimes, a divorced spouse doesn't comply by refusing to add minor children to a work health insurance policy or by refusing to add the former spouse as a beneficiary on a life insurance policy (for the benefit of the minor children). If an ex-spouse is refusing to pay or is underpaying child support, there is another option than returning to court (see "Failure to Pay Child Support" below).

Substantial Change in Circumstances

There is no hard-and-fast rule for what constitutes a "substantial change in circumstances" sufficient to warrant a modification of a final divorce decree. If, for example, your ex-spouse's income increases substantially (perhaps due to a new, higher-paying job), this may warrant a recalculation of the support he is paying. Or if your ex-spouse has joint custody and begins abusing the children (or abusing drugs and alcohol), this may warrant a change from joint to sole custody and a modification of the visitation schedule, since this would be in the children's best interest. Typically, when considering modifications, courts won't reconsider the original division of property or debt, but if the case warrants, they will make modifications to spousal and child support and to custody and visitation.

Note that the same standards apply equally to both parties. Should you earn substantially more or less than what you earned when support was ordered in the final judgment, or should you fail to provide appropriate parenting to your children, be prepared to go back to court.

Janet's situation is a good example. She originally agreed to a 70/30 shared custody plan with her ex-husband. After the divorce decree was entered, he took up with a girlfriend who was trouble. One day, when Janet was dropping off her eleven-year-old son for Saturday visitation, she heard fighting inside the ex-husband's apartment. She could hear screaming, hitting, and what sounded like things being thrown around the apartment. She refused to leave her son and came to me to change the custody arrangement. I went to court on her behalf and was able to establish that the current visitation plan was not in the child's best interest. In order to make the change, we requested a child custody evaluation to look into the mental health and parenting practices of the child's father. Custody and visitation orders are often based on the findings of these evaluations, which could be ordered for a number of reasons, including concerns about child abuse, substance abuse, mental health problems, or questionable parenting practices that could have a negative impact on children. The evaluation is conducted by a qualified mental health professional, such as a psychiatrist, psychologist, qualified social worker, or a marriage and family therapist appointed by the court.

In Janet's case, once the appointed psychologist conducted the evaluation, she prepared a fifty-eight-page report of her conclusions, based on interviewing the mother, father, and child, and visits with the child at each parent's home. Her conclusion was that the boy should spend only limited, supervised visitation with the father and that the father should have weekly visits with a psychologist and undergo psychiatric evaluation before he would have further unsupervised visitation with the son. The court adopted the recommendations of the psychologist.

The important thing to remember when contemplating whether to seek modification of a custody order is that the court will only make changes if 1) it is in the child's best interest, and 2) you can prove it. Even if those two criteria are met, it is often a costly and arduous process to obtain a court-ordered modification.

> **INSIDER TIP**
>
> *Chances are good that your ex-husband will want to avoid going back to court once the divorce decree is final. If you can obtain an agreement to modify the final judgment, you won't have to go back to court. If you know that he is earning substantially more, see if you can negotiate higher support payments on your own. Whatever you agree upon must be documented in writing to be enforceable.*

Failure to Pay Child Support

After you get a child support court order, the other parent must start making child support payments to you. In every case ordering support, the court will order that a wage assignment (garnishment) be issued and served. The wage assignment tells the employer of the person ordered to pay support to take the support payments out of that person's wages.

However, if your former spouse is self-employed or changes jobs frequently, the wage assignment process won't work, and it can be difficult to collect support. In those cases, as long as you have a child support order, you can contact your county's local child support agency (LCSA) and ask them to get involved in the case. They will collect the payments and send them to you. Their services are free of charge.

The LCSA can take income tax returns, they can freeze bank accounts, and they can suspend driver's licenses or other professional licenses (like a contractor's license or a lawyer's license to practice). They can also file papers on behalf of either parent to change the amount of support when there has been a change in income, family status, or something else that would affect the support amount.

When a parent is late or fails to pay court-ordered support payments, the local child support agency can do one or more of these to collect support:

- **Credit reporting:** Not paying child support on time can affect a person's credit rating. The local child support agency will report each child support payment to major credit reporting agencies. They also report the failure to pay child support.
- **Passport denial:** Anytime a person owes more than $2,500 in back child support, the US State Department will not issue or renew a passport until all past-due support payments (also called "arrears") are paid. If your passport application is denied, you will have to make arrangements with the local child support agency to make your child support current before traveling outside the United States. You will also have to make arrangements if your passport needs to be renewed while you are already out of the United States.
- **Property liens:** The LCSA will file a lien against the real property (like a house or land) of a parent who owes

back support. When the property is sold, past-due support may be paid out of the proceeds from the sale.

- **Suspending licenses:** The LCSA can request that any permanent, state-issued license be suspended or withheld to collect back child support. The State Licensing Match System is used to match parents who owe child support with business, professional, and driver's licenses. These licenses include those for cosmetologists, contractors, doctors, teachers, lawyers, and more.

- **Franchise Tax Board child support collection program:** The LCSA must let the Franchise Tax Board know anytime a person is more than $100 and sixty days behind in paying support. The Franchise Tax Board can take funds from bank accounts, rental incomes, royalties, dividends, and commissions. The Franchise Tax Board can also issue an earnings withholding order and take real and personal property, such as vacant land, cash, safe deposit boxes, vehicles, and even boats.

- **Income tax intercepts:** The Internal Revenue Service and the Franchise Tax Board can also intercept tax refunds to pay back child support.

- **Financial institution data match:** Many banks, savings-and-loan institutions, and credit unions in California and the United States report the assets they hold. These assets can be taken for payment of current and back child support.

- **Disability Insurance Benefit Intercept System:** The LCSA can take part of state disability payments owed to parents who owe child support to pay both current and back child support.

- **Unemployment Insurance Benefit Intercept System:** Part of state unemployment benefit payments due to the noncustodial parent can be taken to pay both current and back child support.

- **Workers' Compensation Appeals Board match system:** Lump-sum workers' compensation awards can be taken to pay back child support.
- **Lottery intercept:** Lottery winnings can be taken to pay both current and back child support.

How to Use Social Media to Increase Your Business

In chapter 2, I encourage you to consider starting your own business (see "Be Your Own Boss," page 51). And in chapter 5, I guide you in developing a business plan (see "Launch Your Own Business," page 131). Here, I discuss using social media as an integral part of promotion and sales for any business. Keep these tips in mind as you brainstorm what your business will be and how to make it a success, since social media allows you to quickly and easily get to know your prospects and establish relationships. Even if you haven't yet started your business, familiarize yourself with all the social media tools you'll want to use.

Colleen Francis, a sales expert and president of Engage Selling, says that she has seen salespeople pursue leads using social media and end up with sales of between $30,000 and $250,000. "The biggest sales have come from salespeople using Twitter to find opportunities and LinkedIn to find the names of the true buyers inside organizations," she says. Facebook and blog platforms have proven to be essential for salespeople as well.

For example, a mother in our neighborhood started a successful scrapbooking company by selling digital scrapbooking

> **INSIDER TIP**
> *For a complete tutorial on how to create a Facebook page for your business website, check out ShoutMeLoud (www.shout meloud.com). Facebook has 1.59 billion monthly active users, so your brand needs to be on Facebook. And you can target your specific market at a fraction of the cost of a traditional advertising campaign.*

software and supplies. She connects with her customers on Facebook and through a blog where she shares project ideas and digital photo advice. She publicizes both in person and in virtual scrapbooking Facebook events. She offers an e-newsletter through her blog, and it offers more project ideas. As a result, her existing customers always come back to her for supplies to do the projects she shares, and they also remember her when doing other scrapbook projects. They share her posts with their friends through social networks, leading to still more new customers. She has built a thriving business with both new customers and reordering customers as a result of her online contact with them.

Here are five steps for how *you* can use social media to grow your business.

Step 1: Determine the Best Way to Connect with Prospects

Before joining a social network to make sales, you must know your client base. Social media is a smart selling tool if your clients and prospects are using social media. It's a huge waste of your time if your clients are spending their time elsewhere.

But if you learn they are indeed using popular sites like Facebook, Twitter, and LinkedIn, you need to determine which space is best for connecting and interacting with them. Facebook is one of the best arenas for business-to-consumer sales. It's also important for brands to consider tools like Instagram and Pinterest to increase visibility and sales.

But on any site, you can't simply post products. It's all about engaging with the community, presenting products or services in fun and interesting ways, and offering a collection of images and posts that appeal to the lifestyle of your customers.

LinkedIn is the appropriate platform for sales of business-to-business products or services. LinkedIn is a professional networking environment, so this is the right place to connect with people at corporations.

You can employ Twitter for all kinds of sales. The primary use should be listening, not broadcasting. Use what you hear as leverage to pick up the phone and call. Listen for problems that can be solved.

In addition to the three big social networking sites, blogs, live chats, and comment sections on websites are also great places to generate leads. Salespeople have been successful in blogging about issues related to the problems their products solve and participating in online forums where these topics are discussed. Meeting someone at their point of need, a salesperson can then create a lead who is interested in learning more about a product or service that offers a solution.

No matter what you are selling, you need to find out where your market is having conversations, and go there.

Step 2: Join a Community and Create a Persona

Start by spending some time with the social media tool(s) you plan to use. Build up a personal account, have conversations, and become acquainted with the norms and expectations of the community. This is something you can do even before your business is ready to launch.

Create a persona that's likable and trustworthy within that community. Show your network that you're an amiable, trustworthy resource.

Step 3: Connect

Friend, follow, or connect with individuals with profiles that match those of your potential clients. How do you do this?

Conduct a search on each social networking website or use a resource like Social Mention (www.socialmention.com) to find people who are talking about your industry or using related keywords. Then comment on their posts, retweet them, answer a question, or share something they say. By contributing to their conversation, you add value to their network. Then it becomes natural for you to follow them and for them to follow you back.

Once you connect, don't immediately bombard people with pitches. Instead, read their profiles, get to know them, and identify their needs. When you're ready to approach someone directly, do it privately.

A prescheduled call is often a great tool, but even a private message or email can be a first step where you specifically reference what you've learned about that person through your interactions on social media. Then you don't feel like a pushy salesperson but rather a friend with a specific solution.

Step 4: Build Relationships

The most important thing salespeople need to do, more than develop leads, is to develop relationships because good relationships turn into leads. People share a lot of information, and if you listen to what they say, you will be able to engage in a meaningful conversation with them.

Once you develop a relationship, you can tell the prospect how your product or service might be something they want or need.

Step 5: Engage in a Conversation

If you just write people a message with a pitch and a link to your website, they will be uninterested. If you say, "Here are some solutions to your problem. Maybe my product or service can help," they will know you care about them. The way to persuade is through understanding. If you really listen to what people say on social media, you can open doors and start a conversation without having to make a cold call.

Here are some ways to do this:

- Create a Facebook group related to your product or service and invite prospects to join. Then, send targeted messages to members who are active within the group.

- Join the groups that your clients are members of on LinkedIn. Engage in conversation by answering questions and showcasing your expertise at problem solving in a specific area.
- Twitter also offers opportunities to initiate dialogues. Listen to your prospects' tweets and use them as triggers to start a conversation on a business development call. Look for trends in their tweets. Are they launching new products? Buying new companies? Expanding to a new market? When announcements relate to something you sell, call your prospect, mention the tweet, ask them how it's affecting their business, and see if what you have to offer might help.

If you share good content with your social networks, it can spread easily, increasing your visibility with new leads. You can also give better service when paying attention to customers online, which can result in loyal customers for life.

 Effective Coparenting

More than 40 percent of children are being raised by a divorced parent in the United States. In most cases, the judge orders joint custody of the children. Joint custody requires you to coparent your child with your ex, which means you will be dealing with him for years. Coparenting can give your children stability and close relationships with both parents — but it's rarely easy. In fact, it is usually extremely difficult. Putting aside relationship issues to coparent is challenging, but it can make all the difference in raising happy, healthy kids — and allowing you to get your life on track to a satisfying future.

Especially after a difficult split, it can be extremely challenging to overcome any built-up resentment. Making shared decisions and interacting with each other at drop-offs, the children's school, and sporting events can seem like impossible tasks. But while it's true that coparenting isn't easy, it is the best way to ensure your children's needs are met and they are able to retain close relationships with both parents.

As I've said, how well you handle the conflict of being divorced will make the biggest difference in how well your children handle it. If your ex-husband is not mindful or handling it well, then it is especially important that you do. As our family therapist explained to me when I was going through my divorce, "The children only need one good parent to thrive." Be that parent.

Do your best to coparent with your ex and follow the steps outlined below. However, if all else fails and it is impossible to "coparent" effectively, know that if you stay grounded and mindful, your kids will be fine.

The key to effective parenting after divorce is to focus on your children — and your children only. This means putting aside your own emotions — any anger, resentment, or hurt about the end of your marriage. While this is extremely difficult after a contentious divorce, it is absolutely essential for your and your children's sanity.

I spent five years in court *after* my divorce was "final" litigating the details of the joint custody arrangement. The stress and strain of having to deal with my ex in a courtroom as we litigated where the kids would spend the weekend was damaging to both me and the kids. Every time I had to face my ex in court, I got physically ill.

On the eve of trial, I was driving down the freeway and was struck by a novel idea: *Let it go*. It was as though I'd been struck by a bolt of lightning. I'd fought so long and so hard for years. And here I was, ready to go to trial. But all I could hear was *Let it go*. And I did. I called my ex — the first time we'd talked on the phone in five years — and told him I was taking the trial off the calendar. I was met with dead silence and disbelief. I knew he couldn't believe that I was going to let it go. But I did.

I told the judge that the kids were old enough to decide where they wanted to spend their time. They were teenagers — so it was possible for them to have input. When I let go of the outcome, a remarkable thing happened. My ex showed up more fully for the kids. The kids were happy, and I was happier, too, since they were doing well and now I had some time for myself. This experience, so different from my typical way of trying to control the outcome, was a complete game changer for me.

The way through single parenting is to continually remind yourself that you cannot change your ex. Pick your battles, let go of issues that don't really matter or can't be changed, and accept with grace and maturity the frustrations that typically arise with shared custody — understanding that this is just the reality of divorce.

Divorced mothers express some common frustrations with their ex-husbands: They cancel or are late for pickups; they feed the kids junk food; they don't limit TV or computer time; they buy things the kids don't need instead of necessities like school clothes and shoes; they let kids stay up past their bedtime; and despite having joint custody, they don't take kids to doctor's appointments, dentist's appointments, or extracurricular activities.

These things aren't fair, but they also aren't worth going to court over or even getting upset over. The fact is that unless your ex-husband is abusing the kids or putting them in jeopardy, you can't generally control his actions, and it's a costly endeavor to try.

I'm not suggesting that you be a doormat. Legal action is required if your ex is abusive; some situations warrant going to court. Otherwise, let go of the rest.

Follow these guidelines to remain calm, stay consistent, avoid or resolve conflict with your ex, and make joint custody work.

Separate Your Feelings from Your Behavior

Your feelings don't have to dictate your behavior. Instead, let what's best for your kids — you working cooperatively with your ex-husband — motivate your actions.

GET YOUR FEELINGS OUT SOMEWHERE ELSE

Never vent to your child. This is what your therapist is for and why I suggest you engage in a strong mindfulness practice. Double-down on the mindful practice in chapter 1 (page 26), review the section below on forgiveness ("Be Better, Not Bitter," page 252), and meet regularly with your therapist so that you don't unnecessarily involve your children in adult issues.

STAY KID-FOCUSED

If you feel angry or resentful, try to remember why you need to act with restraint: Your children's best interests are at stake. If your anger feels overwhelming, put a picture of your children at your altar and practice the steps in chapter 1, while focusing on letting go of negative feelings so that you can focus on how you can best meet your children's needs.

NEVER USE KIDS AS MESSENGERS

When you have your children tell the other parent something for you, or worse yet, use your children to collect child support, it puts them in the center of your conflict. The goal is to keep your children out of your relationship issues, so call or email your ex yourself.

KEEP YOUR ISSUES TO YOURSELF

Never say negative things about your ex to your children or make them feel like they have to choose. Your children have a right to a relationship with their other parent that is free of your influence.

Communicating with Your Ex

Peaceful and purposeful communication with your ex is essential to the success of coparenting — even though it may be extremely difficult. *Think about communication with your ex as having the highest purpose: your children's well-being.* Make your children the focal point of every discussion you have with your ex-partner. Remember, this is not about you or your ex — it's about the kids.

It isn't always necessary to meet your ex in person to deal with issues regarding the children — exchanging texts or emails works best for the majority of conversations. The goal is to establish conflict-free communication. Experiment with different forms of communication to figure out what works best for you. One reason I recommend the program Our Family Wizard, especially at the beginning of shared custody, is because it offers divorced parents an accurate, clear log of divorce communication. You will likely find that, as time passes, you can tolerate more frequent and even face-to-face contact. However you communicate, keep the following effective methods in mind.

Set a businesslike tone

Approach the relationship with your ex as you would a business partnership, where your "business" is your children's well-being. Speak or write to your ex as you would a colleague — with respect and neutrality.

Make requests

Instead of making loaded statements, such as, "We really need you to step up and do the right thing and pay for Trevor's soccer club," try framing what you want as requests — as in, "Would you be willing to...?"

Listen

Communicating effectively starts with listening. Listening does not signify approval, so you won't lose anything by allowing your ex to voice his opinion. It simply sets the stage to get what you want.

SHOW RESTRAINT

You can train yourself to not overreact to your ex by taking a deep breath and thinking before speaking, texting, or emailing. Over time you will become numb to the buttons he tries to push.

KEEP CONVERSATIONS KID-FOCUSED

You can control the content of your communication. Never let a discussion with your ex-partner digress into a conversation about your needs or his needs; it should always only be about your children's needs.

CHILL OUT

If a special outing with your ex is going to cut into your time with your children by an hour, let it be. Remember that it's all about what is best for your children. Plus, when you show flexibility, your ex is more likely to be flexible with you.

Parenting as a Team

Coparenting is full of decisions you'll have to make with your ex, whether you like each other or not. Cooperating and communicating without blowups or bickering makes decision-making far easier on everybody. If you shoot for consistency, geniality, and teamwork with your ex, the details of child-rearing decisions tend to fall into place.

It's healthy for children to be exposed to different perspectives and to learn to be flexible, but they also need to know they're living under the same basic set of expectations at each home. Aiming for consistency between your home and your ex's avoids confusion for your children.

While very challenging at the beginning, this becomes easier over time. In practice, I found that I had to engage in what is sometimes referred to as "parallel parenting" when I first divorced. What I mean is, I clearly set the expectations with my children about homework, bedtimes, and behavior in my house, and I didn't try to change what was happening when the kids were at my ex's house. As time went on and the acrimony between me and my ex diminished, we were able to meet over coffee, talk about the kids, and work together to meet their needs. If this is impossible at the beginning of your divorce, I recommend that you be patient with yourself and your ex until things settle.

MAINTAIN SIMILAR RULES IN EACH HOME

Rules don't have to be exactly the same between two households, but if you and your ex-spouse establish generally consistent guidelines, your kids won't have to bounce back and forth between two radically different disciplinary environments. Important lifestyle rules like homework issues, curfews, and off-limit activities should be followed in both households.

FOLLOW SIMILAR DISCIPLINE AND CONSEQUENCES

Try to follow similar systems of consequences for broken rules, even if the infraction didn't happen under your roof. If, for example, your kids have lost TV privileges while at your ex's house, follow through with the restriction at your house. The same can be done for rewarding good behavior.

SET RELIABLE, CONSISTENT SCHEDULES

Where you can, aim for some consistency in your children's schedules. Making meals,

> **INSIDER TIP**
> *If your ex allows the kids to engage in behaviors that put their health and safety at risk (such as have wild, alcohol-fueled parties while in high school) and refuses to work cooperatively with you to create safe and appropriate boundaries, make an appointment with your attorney to determine whether a change in custody or visitation is warranted in order to protect the health, safety, and welfare of the children.*

homework, and bedtimes similar can go a long way toward helping your children adjust to having two homes.

Major Parenting Decisions

You and your ex will need to make some major decisions regarding your children over the years. When important issues come up, be open, honest, and straightforward, which is crucial to both your relationship with your ex and your children's well-being.

MEDICAL NEEDS WHEN KIDS ARE SICK OR INJURED

Effective coparenting can help parents focus on the best medical care for their children, which helps reduce anxiety for everyone. If you share joint legal custody, you are required to decide together on how to address your children's medical needs and must keep each other in the loop, even if you decide to designate one parent to communicate primarily with health-care professionals. Or you may both attend medical appointments together. You cannot, for example, take your daughter to a therapist without obtaining your ex's consent. This is where effective communication facilitates your children's best interest.

HANDLING SCHOOL AND SCHOOL EVENTS

School plays a major role in maintaining a stable environment for your kids. Be sure to let schools and teachers know about changes in your children's living situation. Speak with your ex ahead of time about class schedules, extracurricular activities, and parent-teacher conferences, and be polite to your ex at school or sports events. If you share legal custody, you are required to jointly make decisions about your children's education. You cannot, for example, move your child out of a public school to a private school without your ex's permission. Doing so could land you back in court.

SHARING EXPENSES

The cost of maintaining two separate households can strain your attempts to be effective coparents. Set a realistic budget and keep accurate records for shared expenses. Provide your ex with reimbursable expenses (and documentation) within thirty days after the expense is incurred. Moms complain to me all the time that their ex hasn't reimbursed them for various health and extracurricular expenses they have incurred — but in most cases, the mom held the expenses for many months before submitting. The divorce decree typically provides that reimbursement should happen within thirty days. If you wait to submit your expenses, you run the risk of not being reimbursed.

Handling Disagreements

You and your ex are bound to disagree over certain issues. Keep the following in mind as you try to come to consensus with your ex (and stay out of court).

RESPECT CAN GO A LONG WAY

Simple manners are often neglected after divorce. Being considerate and respectful includes letting your ex know about school events, being flexible about your schedule when possible, and taking his opinion seriously.

KEEP TALKING THROUGH DISAGREEMENTS

If you disagree with your ex about something important, keep communicating about the topic to reach a resolution. Never discuss your differences of opinion with or in front of your children. If you still can't agree, you may need to talk to a third party, like a therapist or mediator. This can be an effective way to avoid going back to court.

> WISE WOMEN KNOW
> *Happiness does not depend on being right.*

Don't sweat the small stuff

If you disagree about important issues like medical care or choice of school for your children, by all means keep the discussion going. But if you want your child in bed by 7:30 PM and your ex says 8 PM, try to let it go and save your energy for the bigger issues.

Be open to compromise

It may not be your first choice, but compromise allows you both to "win" and makes both of you more likely to be flexible in the future.

Making Transitions Easier

Moving from one household to another, whether it happens every few days or just on weekends, can be very hard for children, especially when they're young. Every reunion with one parent is also a separation with the other; each "hello" is also a "good-bye." In joint custody arrangements, transition time is inevitable, but there are many things you can do to help make exchanges and transitions easier, both when your children leave and return.

When your children leave your house

As kids prepare to leave your house for your ex's, try to stay positive and deliver them on time. The following strategies can help make transitions easier:

- **Anticipate change:** Remind kids they'll be leaving for the other parent's house at least a day before the switch. Don't wait until the last minute, as this is disruptive and upsetting for kids of all ages.
- **Double up:** To make packing simpler and make kids feel more comfortable when they are at the other parent's house, have kids keep certain basics — toothbrush, hairbrush, pajamas — at both houses.

- **Pack in advance:** Depending on their age, help children pack their bags well before they leave so that they don't forget anything they'll need. Encourage packing familiar reminders like a special stuffed toy or photograph.

WHEN YOUR CHILDREN RETURN HOME

The beginning of your children's return to your home can be awkward or even rocky. Here are tips for making the transition as smooth as possible:

- **Allow time to adjust:** Try to arrange returns so that you have time for a meal and downtime before school starts. If Sunday evenings are a transition time, try to get your children back by 4 PM if possible, so that you can enjoy a family dinner and have a relaxed bedtime routine before the start of the school/work week. When my children were young and switching between homes, this made all the difference on Monday morning.
- **Keep things low-key:** When children first enter your home, try to have some downtime together — read a book or do some other quiet activity.
- **Allow children space:** Children often need a little time to adjust to the transition. If they seem to need some space, do something else nearby, like prepare dinner.
- **Establish a routine:** Play a game or prepare dinner every time your child returns. Kids thrive on routine — if they know exactly what to expect when they return to you, it can help the transition.

 At Home in Your Home

After your divorce, whether you stay in your family home or relocate to a new one, you need to make your living space your own.

Here is a list of suggestions for how to replace reminders of the past with new things so you can move forward.

- **New bedding:** Replace your old bedding with some new sheets, pillows, and a comforter. If you can, splurge on this. Have a friend help you move the furniture around.

- **New paint:** Repaint your bedroom, and choose something fun and feminine. When I downsized to a smaller home, I painted my new room lavender. It was a daily signal that this was now *my* home, which made a big difference in my mood.

- **New lingerie:** Get yourself some new underwear. You don't have to replace all of it, but definitely replace any lingerie that once held special meaning for you.

- **New jewelry:** Buy a new ring, even if it's for a different finger. Your hand will feel very empty without a wedding ring, and it's fun to have a new ring on your finger.

- **New artwork:** Get rid of artwork that you bought with your spouse and that reminds you of him. Have one of your favorite photos blown up and framed instead.

- **New towels:** Freshen up your bathroom with new towels. This is another place to splurge if you can because towels turn a daily shower into a chance to pamper yourself, even for a moment.

- **New pajamas:** Get rid of your old sleepwear and buy yourself something cute and comfy. A new tank top and soft pajama bottoms can make you feel wonderful.

- **New photographs:** Pack up photos of you and your ex as a couple and store them in the garage or attic. Someday your children may want those pictures, but for now, put them out of sight. However, make sure children have photos in their bedrooms of their father. Kids like to have a reminder that their dad is still their dad.

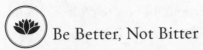 Be Better, Not Bitter

Without forgiveness, you cannot move forward. Forgiveness is not about condoning your ex's bad behavior, but it is about letting go of the hurt that binds you to him. It is the key to moving forward to your new and better life. In my own personal experience, the power of forgiveness has been the single most transformative event in my life.

> WISE WOMEN KNOW
> *"Not forgiving is like drinking rat poison and then waiting for the rat to die."*
> — Anne Lamott

I experienced an extremely high-conflict divorce and a protracted court battle that lasted five years. My children and I spent much of our time in doctors' offices fighting physical and psychological ailments caused by stress. My son had horrible rashes that prevented him from attending school, and I would break out in hives whenever I had to deal with my ex. I feared that the anger and resentment would destroy me and my children, until I experienced the power of true forgiveness.

It happened when I found myself in the location where my ex and I had first fallen in love. I arrived there by accident. My daughter was in a dance team competition in Waikiki over spring break, and the kids and I traveled to the Big Island. The kids and I were having dinner in the hotel, and from where I sat, I could see a Buddha on a point overlooking the ocean. It was lit up in the darkness, and I was drawn to it like a magnet. There was a bench in front of the Buddha, and that was where, twenty-two years before, my husband had kissed me in a way that made me certain we would be together for the rest of our lives. After dinner in the dark, I walked to the point by myself. I sat on the bench beneath the Buddha. I closed my eyes. I was shaking. I remembered how we had fallen in love and started our lives together at this very spot, twenty-two years ago. I marveled at all that had happened during that time: three children, our shared joy, and the pain we caused each other as it all unraveled.

I sat quietly and asked that the anger and resentment be removed so that I could experience joy again.

I opened my eyes. In the darkness in front of me, nestled in the dark lava rock, was a single rosebush and a single pink rose. I was overcome. A feeling unlike anything I have ever experienced filled my entire body. I felt light and free for the first time in five years. Tears streaming down my face, I finally let go of the anger, fear, and pain. Years of anguish were suddenly gone.

When I let go and practiced forgiveness, I experienced a miracle — a complete and dramatic positive change in every aspect of my life. Throughout our separation and divorce, the negative emotions I had been carrying around were eating me alive — and it was contagious. It was as if an illness that was incubating inside of me had infected my children, both psychologically and physically. After I experienced forgiveness, our physical ailments disappeared. My son's rashes were healed. My hives went away. We no longer were spending hours at doctors' offices. Letting go and experiencing forgiveness literally healed me and my children. We all regained our health and vitality.

My life opened up in ways I could never have imagined. I was no longer angry and depleted. My ex and I began to coparent effectively. Our children were laughing again.

Since my energy was positive, I attracted positive people into my life. I began to enjoy life again. I attracted clients and found the freedom to earn a living on my own terms, creating time and space to be available for my children and the things in life that mattered to me. My life was better than it had ever been.

> WISE WOMEN KNOW
> *"True forgiveness is not a lack of discernment or the product of fuzzy thinking. It is the conscious choice to remember the love we experienced, and to let go of anything else.... The fact that I forgive you doesn't mean you 'won.' It doesn't mean you got away with something. It simply means I'm free to go back to the light, reclaim my inner peace, and stay there."*
> — Marianne Williamson

Having let go of the negative thoughts and emotions that had previously filled me, I now had room for love and light. I was better, not bitter. You can be, too.

Take Action to Experience the Healing Power of Forgiveness

- Write a letter to your ex-husband expressing your feelings. This is not a letter that he will read; you are writing this for yourself. Allow yourself to express whatever you are feeling, and let it flow onto the page: hurt, anger, resentment, longing, sadness. The purpose is to purge any toxic emotions you are holding inside you once and for all, so don't hold anything back. When you are done, put the letter in an envelope, seal it, and place it on your altar. Each morning, for seven days, sit in quiet meditation before the altar with the intention of letting go of those negative emotions.
- On the seventh day, burn the letter.
- Sit in quiet meditation and visualize the negative emotions dissipating like the ashes of the letter. Ask that the new space created within yourself be filled with love and light.

My Hope for Readers

As I embarked upon my divorce and then life as a single woman, I never imagined that my life would lead me to where I am now. My ex-husband and I effectively and lovingly coparent our children, the children are happy and grounded, and I enjoy running my legal practice and bringing my ideas of empowerment to women through my work. But getting to this place required navigating tremendous chaos and change. I experienced the perfect storm of loss — the trifecta of grief: the simultaneous loss of my marriage, my father, and my job. The impact of these losses nearly destroyed me.

Having been literally brought to my knees, I experienced a radical transformation. I learned to accept the way things are without casting blame, I asked for help, and I took responsibility for my own actions. Through this process of acceptance and letting go, I was able to practice forgiveness — of others and myself — which set me free. Free to step out of my comfort zone, take appropriate risks, and ultimately take back my power.

As I changed myself, my circumstances began to reflect my newfound strength. My ex and I were at peace. The children were well. The business took off. I experienced the satisfaction of helping others. I began to enjoy life again.

I know that you, too, can be and do whatever you desire. It's never too late to start anew. We are here to experience and enjoy life. If you are not, it's time to make a change.

The time is now. There is an energetic movement of support. Never has it been more timely to *take back your power*.

Acknowledgments

I would like to express my appreciation to the following people who inspired me to share my story and what I have learned on my journey:

Reverend John Calhoun, for seeing my future before I did and encouraging me to follow my path.

Taylor and Ryan Grant, for allowing me to learn from my mistakes and giving me a reason to continue when the going was tough.

My parents, John and Juanita Schuster, for loving me and supporting me.

My clients, whose stories inspired this book, and whose names have been changed to protect their privacy.

Linda Reeves and Kate Deering, for walking along the path of the unknown with me and giving me pep talks along the way.

Jennie Nash, who worked tirelessly with me to create a winning formula.

My agent, Jacqueline Flynn, of Joelle Delbourgo Associates, for being such a great example of enthusiasm and grit.

Georgia Hughes, editorial director of New World Library, for believing in my message of empowerment.

Index

income increases/raises, 207–10

income tax intercepts to pay back child support, 235

individual retirement accounts (IRAs), 196, 197, 204, 230

infidelity, 32–34

insurance provided through the employer, documents regarding, 6

International Association of Women (IAW), 143

investment programs, 6

investments aligned with retirement, 204

IRS (Internal Revenue Service), 141, 229, 235

joint accounts, closing, 228

joint custody, 232, 240, 241, 242, 249

journaling, 28, 160–61

Kia, obtaining credit score from, 50

Kieling, Melissa, 51–52

"Know Your Worth" tool, 207

Kornfield, Jack, 225

Kübler-Ross model, 117. *See also* grieving process

Lamott, Anne, 252

Landers, Ann, 91

land-use permit, 142

lawyer: finding, 15–17; interviewing, 17; questions to ask, 42–44; retaining, with knowledge and information, 41–44. *See also* attorney's fees; divorce financial lawyer; legal issues

LCSA (local child support agency), 234–36

Lebeau, Leslie, 1

legal issues: bullying partner during divorce, handling, 96–100; counsel, retaining with knowledge and information, 41–44; court, avoiding return to, 230–36; divorce decree, preparation of, 194–96; divorce team, building, 14–15; filing for divorce first, 36–37; financial disclosures, preparing, 92–96; icon used for in book, xvii; lawyer, finding, 15–17; mediation, 170–76; narcissistic husband, divorcing, 66–71; negotiating from position of strength, 165–70; notifying husband and serving divorce papers, 64–66; regaining control if husband filed first, 37–41; retirement benefits, dividing, 196–97; temporary support, 124–28; ways to get divorced, 8–14

licenses, for starting your own business, 142

liens, child support and, 234–35

life insurance, 6, 66, 230, 231

LinkedIn, 143, 236, 237, 240. *See also* social media

litigation, traditional, 13–14

LLC (limited liability company), 141

loan statements, 6–7

local child support agency (LCSA), 234–36

lottery intercept, 236

DivorceHacker: An Invitation

*I*f you are interested in receiving additional guidance and support as you navigate divorce and re-create yourself, check out my website, DivorceHacker (www.thedivorcehacker.com). Join our private Facebook group and have your questions answered in a secure and private setting, filled with divorce survivors and the professionals who have guided them. Participate in a workshop and learn about your legal rights, understand the financial issues, and receive compassionate guidance from a lawyer, financial adviser, and therapist. Follow our weekly blog filled with useful tips and inspirational stories of Fearless Females who have used their divorce as a catalyst for positive change. Download the DivorceHacker app to implement the steps outlined in this book and stay on track. Check out DivorceHacker and all it has to offer.

- DivorceHacker: www.thedivorcehacker.com
- Twitter: www.twitter.com/divorcehacker
- Instagram: www.instagram.com/divorcehacker
- Facebook: www.facebook.com/thedivorcehacker

About the Author

$\mathcal{A}$nn Grant didn't aspire to be a divorce lawyer. She was a partner at a large multinational law firm, representing Fortune 500 companies, married to a corporate litigator. They had three children, and life was good. Until it all came to a crashing halt. Over the next five years, Ann went through a devastating divorce that threatened her emotional health and financial stability.

Through the process of letting go and finding forgiveness, Ann took back her life. When it was finally over, she made the decision to commit her career to helping women navigate the legal minefields and outsmart the system so they can get to a new and better life with their sanity intact and their money where it belongs: in the bank.

In her legal practice in Manhattan Beach, California, she helps dozens of women every year. Together with financial advisers and therapists, Ann also runs workshops for women facing divorce, and blogs frequently on the topic.

Ann received her juris doctorate degree from the University of San Diego School of Law, where she graduated cum laude in 1991. While there, she served as editor of the *San Diego Law Review*. She is the former editor of the *Woman Advocate* newsletter, the official publication of the Woman Advocate Committee of the Litigation Section of the American Bar Association, and a former adjunct professor of law at Southwestern University in Los Angeles.